# The Art of Hacking - Ancient Wisdom for Cybersecurity Defense

BY Kenneth May

# Contents

"Just because you're paranoid doesn't mean they aren't after you."

Joseph Heller, Catch-22

# Introduction

## My Background

My journey to the world of Information Security has been an unusual one, that's for sure. My first exposure to the world of computing was through my cousin, who generously passed along to me his old Atari 1040STF home computer. I loved that thing, as basic as it was. From there, I got a 486 DOS PC, which really seemed like a huge step backwards. After that, the family got a 75 Mhz Pentium PC from Hewlett Packard, and now we were really cooking with fire! At that point, I built my first computer with the help of a couple dear friends. I remember to this day, trying to figure out why it would power up then immediately shut off only to discover we needed to add a heatsink and fan!

I started off my college education at Thomas Aquinas College, tucked away in the mountains of Ojai, California. A small Liberal Arts college, I attended because I wanted to study the great classics of Western Civilization. I wanted to build critical thinking skills and understand the history of the world around me a bit better. I started picking up random consulting jobs, just being a techie, and during my first summer break, I got a job working for a UPS support contractor. It was a call center job, supporting their primary shipping software. During our two-week training class, I would wind up being asked to teach part of the class! It was a really grueling job, however. My next summer, I got a job working for Best Buy, before they started the whole Geek Squad thing. After meeting a customer that convinced me to start consulting, since Best Buy would not do house calls at the time, I was on my path.

It was around this time that I became very interested in Chinese Martial Arts. I had been practicing for a few years, but I met my first real Sifu (teacher/Shifu/Sensei). Because of my interest in Chinese culture, and the fact that I had several people near and dear to me who had illnesses that western medicine could not help, I decided to go into Acupuncture and Chinese Herbal Medicine. I had a friend through Kung Fu classes who had enrolled at the Santa Barbara College of Oriental Medicine, and I decided to sign up for their Masters Degree program.

This was a pretty amazing experience. I wound up being the only student in my class to elect to study abroad in both Japan and China. I also wound up apprenticing with a fantastic doctor in Chinatown. Fantastic memories, and many incredible experiences. Sadly, right as I was finishing up my schoolwork, the college went out of business. I was in the last graduating class and received my Master of Science Degree in Oriental Medicine. I then set up shop in my little town as an herbalist while I waited until I could take my Acupuncture Board exams. Right about this time, I was offered a job as a fulltime systems administrator by a prior client. This was really a conundrum. Here I just spent three and a half years in college for Acupuncture and had just opened my practice. However, my wife was expecting our first child, and between the salary and full medical and 401k benefits, I determined it would take me five to ten years to build a private practice to that point. After a lot of thinking, a lot of praying, and seeking advice from my mentors, I decided to take the job. Nine months later, the economy tanks, my wife is in the hospital, and I get laid off. Do I go back to school, somewhere in Los Angeles to re-prep for the Acupuncture Board Exam? Or do I go back into consulting?

Well, within a week, I was making money consulting.

I eventually picked up a job as a sub-sub-sub-contractor. I kept going up the food chain until I found someone interested in hiring me for more work. The top-level company was based out of Los Angeles, and really needed a technician. They only had two employee owners: one just there for the money, and one just there for the tech work.

Exit money guy, and now we have a tech trying to run a business. Fast forward a bit, and the company is tanking. Invoices are going out 6-9 months late, and the new sales manager that had been brought on and I were owed a lot of back pay. Well, there was just too much potential here to waste. The sales manager and I approached the remaining owner and had an interesting idea: sell the company to us for what you owe us in back pay, we will hire you as an engineer, and handle turning this thing around. It worked! I rebuilt us as a Managed IT Services Provider, and my new business partner and I were thereafter enjoying high double-digit growth, every year so far. At the time of writing this, we have been an MSP for going on ten years now.

My journey into Information Security has been extremely enjoyable and exciting. As a member of CompTIA's Information Security Community's Executive Council, and teaching as a Community Instructor for SANS, I'm constantly learning from my students and peers. I have found this to be incredibly invaluable to me as I work on various Penetration Testing, forensic, and other cybersecurity projects.

## Change is in the air

So here we are. Business every day are being attacked by hackers, script-kiddies[1] and even state-sponsored teams.[2] In fact, a 2016 report by Symantec claims that 43% of phishing[3] campaigns target small businesses now[4]. What is a business owner to do? Smaller businesses do not have the technical staff or budgets to respond appropriately, and enterprises may be so large and convoluted, that their own internal teams cannot handle it all. This book does not seek to provide detailed technical instructions on attack and defense techniques. Rather, this book is somewhat more philosophical in nature. Our predecessors, both ancient and modern, amassed much wisdom that has been passed own to us through the ages. It would be just as impossible for them to have imagined how this wisdom might apply to our current times, as it is for me to

---

[1] In programming and hacking culture, a script kiddie is an unskilled individual who uses scripts or programs developed by others to attack computer systems and networks and deface websites.

[2] See https://www.cnet.com/news/rule-41-you-cant-hide-from-government-hacking-warrant/, or https://www.eff.org/deeplinks/2016/12/year-government-hacking

[3] Phishing is the attempt to obtain sensitive information such as usernames, passwords, and credit card details (and, indirectly, money), often for malicious reasons, by disguising as a trustworthy entity in an electronic communication.

[4] https://smallbiztrends.com/2016/04/cyber-attacks-target-small-business.html

imagine what our society will be like in 1,000 years. And, that's coming from a Science-Fiction fan.

Certainly, Musashi, Sun Tzu or Publius Flavius Vegetius Renatus would not have believed the esoteric way in which I intend to apply their wisdom here.

I will be drawing from many sources, including authors who lived in China, Japan, Rome and more. While I will annotate terms as much as possible, I will also include a glossary of jargon, in case the technical terms start getting overwhelming.

Where possible, I will give both the translation I am drawing from, if not my own, as well as the source in the original tongue and script. There are so many subtleties that do not always come across in translation, that I always prefer to be able to muddle through the original source myself, where I can, so I offer it here for you as well. I am drawing from so many different sources, I will do my best to properly attribute everything. Please note that if I have missed an attribution somewhere, or have improperly quoted a source, I will endeavor to correct and revise as necessary.

I would also like to note here, that theoretically, much of this book could be used by malicious entities for devising attacks, and defense against detection. However, I am of the mindset that bringing potential vulnerabilities, strategies, and tactics into the open provides a far better landscape of defense than ignorance does. Everything I describe here has happened already, whether by chance or intention. Only by knowing the possible risks can we defend adequately against them.

Many of these great works are more focused on the attack, than on the defense but as they say, sometimes the best defense is a good offense. There is much more wisdom to be absorbed than I reference in this book, and that is only because this work is more focused on the defense of an information system or data network, but I highly encourage the reader to explore these authors more deeply. Techniques or weapons are tools and can be used for both protection and attack. How you use them is up to you, but we should not remain ignorant of their operation lest we become helpless against them.

To access the companion music album *"Music to Hack By"*

Please visit http://music.kenmay.net/

# The Earliest Hackers

No one would fault you for thinking that hacking is purely a modern nuisance. After all, early computers were the size of a city block within our lifetimes, right? Well, the hacker mindset is nothing new. In fact, all the way back in 1792, in France, a gentleman by the name of Claude Chappe created what was arguably one of the first national data networks. A precursor to the electric telegraph, Chappe's semaphore telegraphs were accomplished by setting up relay towers, around 5 to 20 miles apart in line of sight sections, depending on the geography and visibility. These mechanical telegraph towers used systems of adjustable wooden arms, or paddles.

The position of each of these arms would signify different characters in a message to be sent. The operator of the next tower would be on watch for a change, and then he would reconfigure his tower to match. In this way, messages could be passed along in a similar manner to flag semaphore messages, but much more quickly, and across much greater distances. One could send a message from one side of France to the other in a matter of minutes, when traditional courier methods would normally take days, even by horseback!

Now, this system was supposed to only be used for government purposes, such as wartime intelligence. But as we all know, where there is a will, there is a way. In 1834, François and Joseph Blanc, two bankers from Bordeaux, saw an opportunity for personal gain here.

These fine gentlemen traded government bonds at the exchange in their hometown. Now, just as today, traders who could get information about what was happening in the French business world the quickest would be able to make more shrewd trades than their counterparts. Some of these messages included the prime interest rate, which was quite valuable data. The mail could take five days to get from one side of France to the other, so some folks tried horseback messengers and even carrier pigeons to beat their rivals. And so, the Blanc brothers began bribing a telegraph operator in the nearby city of Tours to deliberately corrupt messages passing through.

5

You see, this particular system also included a kind of backspace symbol that instructed the tower operator to ignore the previous character that had been transmitted. It was intended to indicate if the prior character was a mistake. However, they realized that they could add a secret character to the messages, then add the delete character, so that the printed message would come out the same, but someone actually observing the messaging as it was happening could interpret that extra character, which could be used to indicate

[5] Image from Radio News magazine, Ziff-Davis Publishing Co., Inc., New York, Vol. 32, No. 5, November 1944, p. 71

the direction of the markets. To do this, they also needed a co-conspirator out of their local tower, who would then pass the information on to them.

It was not until 1836 when the operator in Tours became extremely sick and confessed his extracurricular activities to a dear friend, who he had intended to take his place. In 1837, the brothers were put on trial and were acquitted, as there were no laws on the books for them to be charged with private use of the telegraph system. Does that scenario sound familiar? The early hackers of the 70s, 80s, and even 90s found themselves in very similar situations.

Let's jump ahead to 1903. Guglielmo Marconi, an Italian man who pioneered the radio, had started a series of public performances in order to showcase his technology[6]. A physicist by the name of John Ambrose Fleming was preparing to give the presentation in person to a large crowd of curious spectators at the Royal Institution's famous lecture theatre in London. Meanwhile, around 300 miles away in Poldhu, Cornwall, Marconi was preparing to send a signal to London from his location on the cliff sides. Mere minutes before Fleming was supposed to receive Marconi's Morse messages, there came an odd, rhythmic ticking noise coming out from the theatre's brass projection lantern, which was used to display the lecturer's slides. To the untrained ear, it sounded like a mechanical issue with the projector. But Arthur Blok, Fleming's assistant, quickly recognized this as the

---

[6] *New Scientist* Magazine, 24 December 2011

uneven tapping of a human hand keying in a message in Morse code. Blok suddenly realized that someone was trying to beam powerful electrical pulses into the theater, and they were clearly strong enough to interfere with the projector's electric arc discharge lamp.

Blok translated the message as a single word "Rats," coming in repeatedly, over and over again. From there it got worse. Much worse. Up next was a charming limerick, which trolled thusly:

*"There was a young fellow of Italy, who diddled the public quite prettily,"*

After that, came additional rude epithets, and oddly, quotes from Shakespeare.

Keep in mind that, previously, Marconi had reassured the public that his wireless messages could be sent completely privately, claiming:

*"I can tune my instruments so that no other instrument that is not similarly tuned can tap my messages.*[7]*"*

Clearly, this was not the case. Marconi and Fleming were quite upset, and called the interference "scientific hooliganism", and "an outrage against the traditions of the Royal Institution". Only four days later, a man by the name of Nevil Maskelyne was quite pleased to confess to the hack. You see, Maskelyne had a lot of 'entrepreneurial' ideas about how to use wireless technology but was constantly frustrated by Marconi's extremely broad patents. Maskelyne used it for mind-

---

[7] *St. James Gazette,* London, 1903

reading tricks with an accomplice, sent wireless messages between a ground station and a balloon 10 miles away, and even used it to remotely ignite gunpowder. Needless to say, he was not a Marconi fan.

Now, there was an all-out monopoly in place by the wired telegraphy companies, and Marconi was threatening to disrupt their entire industry. These companies already had a ton of infrastructure in place, including undersea cables and a small navy to lay and service all these cables.

Thus, the Eastern Telegraph Company, one of the largest of these companies, decided to hire Maskelyne to see if he could prove that Marconi's technology was not everything it claimed to be. And so it was that Maskelyne built a 50 meter tall radio antenna on the cliffs of Porthcurno. The goal being to see if he could listen in on the messages Marconi was sending as part of his ship-to-ship messaging business, which was doing quite well. Maskelyne was happy to announce that:

*"I received Marconi's messages with a 25-foot collecting circuit [aerial] raised on a scaffold pole. When eventually the mast was erected the problem was not interception but how to deal with the enormous excess of energy.[8]"*

---

[8] *The Electrician*, 11/07/1902

Marconi had argued that his transmitter broadcasting on a specific frequency meant that no one else could listen in, unless they had an identical device. At least to my generation, my parents, and my grandparents' generations (but thanks to the digital revolution, most likely to few folks moving forward!), we are familiar with how easy it is to tune an analog radio from station to station. Maskelyne's untuned broadband receiver was able to receive all of these signals with ease. After discovering this, Maskelyne realized all he needed was a simple transmitter to send messages on the same frequency, and he was fully capable of interfering surreptitiously.

Maskelyne then chose to stage his hack of the Royal Institution by setting up his transmitter and Morse key at his father's music hall in the nearby West End.

Maskelyne easily could have sent his messages at the same time as Marconi and would have caused them to be all received together, which would have been printed out mindlessly during the demo. By choosing to make his messages separate and obvious, only Marconi and Fleming knew what was happening at the time, and only Marconi and Fleming made the public aware by all their blustering.

We see nearly the same issues occur to this day. Ethical hackers and developers privately disclose vulnerabilities they have found to the authors, so they have time to fix the code before it is widely exploited. Ideally, the vendors and code authors pay out on some kind of a bug bounty system to encourage this – with the threat of public disclosure if no action is taken.

But let us go further back into the rich history of brilliant philosophers, generals, and thought-leaders, and see what their wisdom still has to share.

# 1. Thucydides - History of the Peloponnesian War

Thucydides was an Athenian general, "the father of political history," and a talented analyst of power, chance, and necessity in international affairs. Perhaps his best-known work, the *History of the Peloponnesian War* recalls the war between Sparta and Athens (435–411 BCE) and was intended to be "a possession for all times."

Very little is passed down to us about his life except what he shared with us through his own works. We learn from *The History of the Peloponnesian War* that he was a general who saw combat in the war[9], that he contracted the deadly plague that afflicted Athens some time between 430 and 427, that he would be the one to slay Pericles[10], and that he was eventually exiled by the democracy for his failure to save the city of Amphipolis from the forces of Sparta[11].

---

[9] History of the Peloponnesian War, 4.104.4; 4.105.1

[10] Ibid, 2.48.3; 3.87.3

[11] Ibid, 5.26.5

About his background, he shares with us:

*"The general who had come from Athens to defend the place, sent to the other commander in Thrace, Thucydides son of Olorus, the author of this history, who was at the isle of Thasos, a Parian colony, half a day's sail from Amphipolis[12]".*

Whether it is entirely factual or not, *The History of the Peloponnesian War* is generally considered one of the earliest Western scholarly works of history.

## Book I – The Search for Truth

*"οὕτως ἀταλαίπωρος τοῖς πολλοῖς ἡ ζήτησις τῆς ἀληθείας, καὶ ἐπὶ τὰ ἑτοῖμα μᾶλλον τρέπονται."*

*"So averse to taking pains are most men in the search for the truth, and so prone are they to turn to what lies ready at hand. [13]"*

Even in the time of Thucydides, we see a common thread of human behavior. Mankind seems far more likely to accept a convenient truth than to put forth the effort required to test the veracity of any given statement. Hackers know this and can use this trait to convince people to act in a way they want.

---

[12] Ibid, 1.104.4

[13] Ibid, 1.20-[3]

In reference to Information Security, Social Engineering can possibly be described as the psychological manipulation of people into performing certain actions or divulging confidential information[14].

In 1894, Dutch industrialist Jacques van Marken (1845-1906) used in one of his essays the term "social engineers" (sociale ingenieurs), proposing the idea that modern employers needed the assistance of specialists in handling the human problems of the planet, just as they needed technical expertise (ordinary engineers) to deal with the problems of dead matter (materials, machines, processes). An 1897 summary of this call, by English economist Henry Wolff thus states:

*"M. van Marken perceived that there was much amiss in the social world which called for amendment, and he became the first avowed 'Christian socialist' of his country. The harvest was, however, too great for one husbandman. So, he pleaded for a new calling to be taken up by public-spirited men: a calling which ho christened 'social engineering.' There are some 'social engineers' at work now, and they are reaping results.[15]"*

The bigger picture is that, whatever term you use, people have been exploiting this behavior across cultures for many millennia, and humanity is not likely changing this behavior any time soon. Knowing this, we must ensure that we have adequate compensating

---

[14] https://en.wikipedia.org/wiki/Social_engineering_(security)

[15] Wolff, Henry W. (1897). "Article", *The Economic Review* (pg. 122), Volume 7.

protections in place to anticipate potential breaches of policy due to manipulation of internal staff by social engineering.

Robert Cialdini[16] proposes six key principles of his theory of influence:

1. **Reciprocity** – People are very likely to return a favor, so one can see the pervasiveness of free samples in marketing. Cialdini, during his conferences, has been known to use the example of Ethiopia providing thousands of dollars in humanitarian aid to Mexico just after the 1985 earthquake, despite Ethiopia enduring a brutal famine and civil war at the same time. Ethiopia had until this point been retuning in kind the diplomatic support that Mexico had provided when Italy invaded Ethiopia in 1935. The good cop/bad cop stratagem is also based on this sort of principle.

2. **Commitment and consistency** – If people commit themselves, whether verbally or in writing, to an idea or goal, then they are much more likely to honor that commitment since they have stated that that idea or goal fits well their self-image. In fact, even if the original incentive or motivation becomes removed after they have already agreed, they will still continue to honor the previous agreement. Cialdini in his writings mentions the

---

[16] Robert Beno Cialdini (born April 27, 1945) is the Regents' Professor Emeritus of Psychology and Marketing at Arizona State University and was a visiting professor of marketing, business and psychology at Stanford University, as well as at the University of California at Santa Cruz, best known for his 1984 book on persuasion and marketing, *Influence: The Psychology of Persuasion*.

supposed Chinese "brainwashing" of American PoWs to re-create their own self-image and thus gain automatic unenforced compliance. Yet another example would be the marketers who force the user to close popups with the only option saying, "I'll sign up later" or "No thanks, I prefer not making money".

3. **Social proof** – People will often do things they see other people are doing. For example, in one experiment, one or more of his researchers would look up at the sky. Then, bystanders would look up to the sky to see what they were missing. Eventually, this experiment had to be stopped because so many bystanders were looking up that they stopped traffic. See the Asch conformity experiments for further reference.

4. **Authority** – People will naturally tend to obey figures of authority - even if they are asked to do objectionable acts. Cialdini quotes incidents such as the infamous Milgram experiments that occurred in the early 1960s and the My Lai massacre.

5. **Liking** – People can be easily persuaded by other people that they like. Cialdini mentions the marketing of Tupperware in what we might now call viral marketing. People were much more likely to buy the product, if they liked the person selling it to them. Some of the many biases that favor those more attractive people are discussed: see discussions on physical attractiveness stereotypes for more information.

6. **Scarcity** – Perceived scarcity will generate demand. For example, those ads which say offers are available for a "limited time only" encourages greater sales.

## Book I – Acting in War

"ἰόντες τε οἱ ἄνθρωποι ἐς τοὺς πολέμους τῶν ἔργων πρότερον ἔχονται, ἃ χρῆν ὕστερον δρᾶν, κακοπαθοῦντες δὲ ἤδη τῶν λόγων ἅπτονται."

*"It is a common mistake in going to war to begin at the wrong end, to act first, and wait for disaster to discuss the matter.[17]"*

Sadly, I see this play out regularly. I am contacted by a company who has experienced a major security breach, and they have either very little security infrastructure in place, or it is completely random, and doesn't follow any sort of Standards or guidelines. Barring an explicit compliance or regulatory requirement, there should always be some sort of pre-planned and thoroughly discussed plan of action. One approach may be to apply something like the Center for Internet Security's Top 20 Security Controls[18].

According to the Center for Internet Security: *"The CIS Critical Security Controls are informed by actual attacks and effective defenses and*

---

[17] History of the Peloponnesian War, Book I, 1.78.2-4

[18] https://www.cisecurity.org/controls

*reflect the combined knowledge of experts from every part of the ecosystem (companies, governments, individuals); with every role (threat responders and analysts, technologists, vulnerability-finders, tool makers, solution providers, defenders, users, policy-makers, auditors, etc.); and within many sectors (government, power, defense, finance, transportation, academia, consulting, security, IT) who have banded together to create, adopt, and support the Controls. Top experts from organizations pooled their extensive first-hand knowledge from defending against actual cyber-attacks to evolve the consensus list of Controls, representing the best defensive techniques to prevent or track them. This ensures that the Controls are the most effective and specific set of technical measures available to detect, prevent, respond, and mitigate damage from the most common to the most advanced of those attacks.[19]"*

The Controls include:

**Basic CIS Controls**

1. Inventory and Control of Hardware Assets

2. Inventory and Control of Software Assets

3. Continuous Vulnerability Management

4. Controlled Use of Administrative Privileges

---

[19] https://www.sans.org/critical-security-controls/guidelines

5. Secure Configuration for Hardware and Software on Mobile Devices, Laptops, Workstations and Servers

6. Maintenance, Monitoring and Analysis of Audit Logs

**Foundational CIS Controls**

7. Email and Web Browser Protections

8. Malware Defenses

9. Limitation and Control of Network Ports, Protocols and Services

10. Data Recovery Capabilities

11. Secure Configuration for Network Devices, such as Firewalls, Routers and Switches

12. Boundary Defense

13. Data Protection

14. Controlled Access Based on the Need to Know

15. Wireless Access Control

16. Account Monitoring and Control

**Organizational CIS Controls**

17. Implement a Security Awareness and Training Program

18. Application Software Security

19. Incident Response and Management

20. Penetration Tests and Red Team Exercises

It is well worth researching a Standard of Information Security that best fits your organization, and use that to begin to plan things out even if it is far after the fact, rather than be trapped in a continually reactive mode.

## Book I - LXXXIII - Arms or money?

"εἰσὶ γὰρ καὶ ἐκείνοις οὐκ ἐλάσσους χρήματα φέροντες ξύμμαχοι, καὶ ἔστιν ὁ πόλεμος οὐχ ὅπλων τὸ πλέον, ἀλλὰ δαπάνης, δι᾽ ἣν τὰ ὅπλα ὠφελεῖ..."

"...For they also have allies not less numerous than ours who pay tribute; and war is a matter not so much of arms as of money, for it is money alone that makes arms serviceable...[20]"

An unfortunate reality I regularly come across is that sometimes, despite doing everything correctly, and having a clear understanding of the extant security weaknesses, sacrifices must be made due to a lack of budget. Luckily, this continues to improve. Worldwide, IT security spending in 2019 was expected to grow 8.7 percent over the numbers from 2018 according to a recent Gartner forecast. Cybersecurity

---

[20] History of the Peloponnesian War, 1.83.1-3

Ventures had made predictions that globally cybersecurity spending will be in excess of $1 trillion cumulatively from 2017 to 2021. Of course, all these predictions did not account for the complexities that the Covid-19 virus would bring to the world's economy.

Chief Information Security Officers are sitting closer to the C-Suite than ever before. While there is still a divide between CISOs and other executives, this gap has become narrower. In fact, PwC has noted[21] that the majority of CEOs tend agree that cybersecurity risks are a threat to their organization's entire growth prospects, and according to BDO[22], around a third of all executive board members are briefed on enterprise cybersecurity at least once each quarter.

CISOs and those nontechnical executives on the board will have different priorities for the cybersecurity budget, however. It seems that now most executives view regulations and compliance as key influencers for cybersecurity spending. Business decision-makers must also be concerned that they are making sure security investments which address digital business risks, according to Gartner[23].

---

[21] https://www.pwc.com/us/en/library/ceo-agenda/pdf/21st-annual-global-ceo-survey-us-supplement.pdf

[22] https://www.bdo.com/news/2017-september/bdo-usa-survey-on-cyber-governance-reveals-continu

[23] https://www.gartner.com/en/newsroom/press-releases/2019-03-05-gartner-identifies-the-top-seven-security-and-risk-ma

Meanwhile, the majority of data breaches are caused by people or process failures. Mutual conversations regarding risk and budget can truly help businesses work toward a far more effective security culture and shared risk goals. CISOs must be prepared to find ways to justify their spending by addressing the gaps in the existing security environment. BCG[24] has recommended using these following three topics to guide inter-disciplinary budget talks:

- What is our appetite for risk?

- Where will the investments make biggest impacts?

- How can we get value from our existing investments?

CISOs must be prepared to address the situations where tools or solutions do not translate easily into capabilities or reduced risk. Even more importantly, they must also be ready to address the reasons why some prior investments did not pay off. These discussions may be an opportunity to make a compelling business case for an integrated security ecosystem. Only 39 percent of businesses think they have achieved effectively strong automation and interoperability between key security and incident response processes according to SANS[25].

---

[24] https://www.bcg.com/publications/2019/are-you-spending-enough-cybersecurity.aspx

[25] https://www.sans.org/press/announcement/2019/03/13/1

"αἰεὶ δὲ ὡς πρὸς εὖ βουλευομένους τοὺς ἐναντίους ἔργῳ παρασκευαζόμεθα· καὶ οὐκ ἐξ ἐκείνων ὡς ἁμαρτησομένων ἔχειν δεῖ τὰς ἐλπίδας, ἀλλ' ὡς ἡμῶν αὐτῶν ἀσφαλῶς προνοουμένων. πολύ τε διαφέρειν οὐ δεῖ νομίζειν ἄνθρωπον ἀνθρώπου, κράτιστον δὲ εἶναι ὅστις ἐν τοῖς ἀναγκαιοτάτοις παιδεύεται."

*"In practice we always base our preparations against an enemy on the assumption that his plans are good; indeed, it is right to rest our hopes not on a belief in his blunders, but on the soundness of our provisions. Nor ought we to believe that there is much difference between man and man, but to think that the superiority lies with him who is reared in the severest school.[26]"*

We must not assume that the enemy is ignorant, or is not well trained, or that they will make a fatal mistake. *Sed contra*, we must assume that the enemy will follow the most perfect path and strike where we are weakest. Adversaries will invest a great deal of time and resources into researching and learning about an organization's weak points or vulnerabilities. These weak points could also be some of their recent acquisitions, or seemingly harmless third-party suppliers with extensively unneeded levels of access to their target's systems, or of course, specific types of software and their inherent security flaws.

---

[26] History of the Peloponnesian War, Book I, 1.84-[4]

Much of this type of information can be gathered through OSINT (Open-Source Intelligence) sources. This method is pulling data and metadata from publicly available information, such as social media, DNS, the organization's website, and other similar sources.

Thus, defensive cybersecurity specialists should apply the same rigor in understanding the adversary and their tactics. This understanding may also aid in defining the organization's unique threat environment. It might be embodied in internal teams which are focused on outward research, working together with a reputable cyber threat intelligence vendor and, more and more, sharing their threat intelligence with their peers, other industry groups and the government itself through Information Sharing and Analysis Organizations (ISAOs).

## Book IV – Careless Hope

"καὶ γὰρ καὶ ἄδεια ἐφαίνετο αὐτοῖς, ἐψευσμένοις μὲν τῆς Ἀθηναίων δυνάμεως ἐπὶ τοσοῦτον ὅση ὕστερον διεφάνη, τὸ δὲ πλέον βουλήσει κρίνοντες ἀσαφεῖ ἢ προνοίᾳ ἀσφαλεῖ, εἰωθότες οἱ ἄνθρωποι οὗ μὲν ἐπιθυμοῦσιν ἐλπίδι ἀπερισκέπτῳ διδόναι, ὃ δὲ μὴ προσίενται λογισμῷ αὐτοκράτορι διωθεῖσθαι"

"...and their judgment was based more upon blind wishing than upon any sound prediction; for it is a habit of mankind to entrust to careless *hope what they long for, and to use sovereign reason to thrust aside what they do not desire.[27]"*

Hope and fear should not architect our networks. Quite often this is the case, when looking at the budgets for IT departments. For example, in *"Between Hope and Fear: The Psychology of Risk[28]"*, the author explains to us:

*"A simple truth: you can't have it all."*

A corollary is: you want more than you can have. It seems that conflict itself is in the nature of all living things. All available resources are limited, such as wealth, time, and food, so people get plenty of practice juggling inconsistent desires and cobbling together tolerable compromises.

Conflict itself arises in two places here. The first is the conflict existing between security and potential. It goes without saying in the investment world that risk and return go together. If you want to have safety, you must pay for it in yield; if you want to have yield you must pay for it in worry. To say that "security/potential" defines a dispositional variable here is to say that people will typically just choose one way or the other between avoiding perceived bad outcomes and approaching what they see as good outcomes. But this does not mean that people do not perceive at all what they do not choose. When making an obvious decision for security, a person may absolutely regretfully acknowledge

---

[27] History of the Peloponnesian War, Book IV, 4.108-[4]

[28] https://doi.org/10.1016/S0065-2601(08)60416-5

their loss of opportunities. People also are very quick to notice the special benefits granted from choices such as a riskless lottery that allows them to have their cake and eat it too.

The second form of conflict is both more interesting and less obvious. These are the conflicts that can be created as different situations induce different patterns of agreement and disagreement between dispositional motives toward security or potential and the immediate needs and opportunities affecting aspiration level.

Consider someone who is dispositionally motivated to achieve security and suppose that, in the present task situation, the person has a modest aspiration level, say $50. Faced with the choice between the short shot and the long shot, the person would tend to reject the long shot on both counts: it is clearly less secure in Lorenz curve[29] terms and it is also less likely to satisfy the aspiration level. The same would be true for almost any pair of gain lotteries. This is because there is a positive correlation between the ordering of the lotteries in terms of security

---

[29] The Lorenz curve is a graph showing the proportion of overall income or wealth assumed by the bottom x% of the people, although this is not rigorously true for a finite population. It is often used to represent income distribution, where it shows for the bottom x% of households, what percentage (y%) of the total income they have. The percentage of households is plotted on the x-axis, the percentage of income on the y-axis. It can also be used to show distribution of assets. In such use, many economists consider it to be a measure of social inequality. (Wikipedia)

and the ordering of the lotteries in terms of the probability that they will achieve the aspiration level.

For losses, however, there is a conflict between security and aspiration. Consider the same person choosing between the same two lotteries, but this time for losses, and suppose that the aspiration level is to lose no more than $50. The short shot is obviously more secure since its losses are capped at $130, but it is much less likely to yield a loss of $50 or less. This would be true for almost any pair of loss lotteries: the ordering on security runs essentially opposite to the ordering on aspiration level.

For a potential motivated person, the situation would be just reversed. For losses, potential and aspiration level are positively correlated but for gains they are quite likely to be negatively correlated.

Conflict between security/potential and aspiration can produce quite complex patterns of data[30].

To sum up, the two-factor theory integrates a dispositional tendency to seek either security or potential with situationally driven aspiration levels. Security motivation captures the Bernoullian (1967) intuition that people are generally disposed to prefer sure things and gambles without large chances of bad outcomes. However, the theory handles equally directly the less prevalent tendency of some people to approach long shots and other gambles offering the unlikely possibility of large

---

[30] See Coombs & Avrunin, 1983, for a general discussion of data patterns produced by conflict.

outcomes. In addition, the theory deals directly with situational circumstances that may cause a person to experience conflict between dispositionally driven preferences and externally driven goals. Thus, the theory explains how the person can be risk averse in the economic sense (i.e., typically preferring sure things) but sometimes make the same choices as someone who is ordinarily risk seeking.

Understanding the motivations is the easy part. The difficult part is working to convince the powers that be to work logically, and with advice of professionals, rather than go by emotionally motivated decisions.

## 2. Traditional Chinese Idioms

Chinese culture is one of the oldest cultures in the world with extant written works. Boasting historical records and stories going back 5,000 years or more[31], there is a vast selection of great works to draw from. Along with specific books, we have a very rich tradition of idioms available to us. Folk wisdom is often delightfully insightful and to the point, and so I have selected a few of them here that are pertinent to our discussion.

---

[31] https://www.theguardian.com/world/2013/jul/10/inscriptions-predate-oldest-chinese-language

## As precarious as a stack of eggs[32]

## (危如累卵 Wēi Rú Lěi Luǎn)

*"In the Spring and Autumn Period[33], the ruler of the state of Jin gave*
*an order to build a nine-story terrace as a pleasure resort. The*
*construction had taken three years and was still far from being*
*completed. Moreover, it was depleting the manpower and financial*
*resources of the state. Despite this, the ruler of Jin declared, "He who*
*dares to remonstrate shall be executed." Having heard of this, one of*
*the courtiers of Jin, one Xun Xi, requested an audience. The ruler*
*granted him the interview angrily and sat on his throne with a bow*
*and arrow in hand. Xun Xi said, "I dare not to try to dissuade Your*
*Highness, but I wish to show you how I can pile up 12 chess pieces[34]*
*one upon another, and add furthermore nine eggs, one on top pf the*
*other, on top of them." The ruler of Jin replied, "Please demonstrate."*
*Xun Xi then calmed himself and focused his mind. He piled up the*
*chess pieces as he had said, and then put nine eggs on top of them,*
*one on top of the other. All the onlookers held their breath in*

---

[32] *The Stories Behind 100 Chinese Idioms, Sinolingua, 1998, pg. 54*

[33] https://www.britannica.com/event/Spring-and-Autumn-Period : in Chinese
history, the period during the Zhou dynasty (1046–256 bc)—specifically the
first portion of the Dong (Eastern) Zhou—when many vassal states fought and
competed for supremacy. It was named for the title of a Confucian book of
chronicles, Chunqiu, covering the period 722–479 bc.

[34] Keep in mind, this is a Chinese Chess set, not a western Chess set.

*suspense. The ruler was so nervous that he felt suffocated. "That is most precarious," he exclaimed. Xun Xi replied, "No, this is not really precarious. There is something even more precarious than this." He continued, "It has taken three years so far to build the nine-story terrace for Your Highness, and it is still not complete. Men have given up farming, and women have stopped weaving. The manpower and financial resources of the state are virtually exhausted. Consequently, neighboring states are preparing to take advantage of our weakness. Our state is about to perish. What could be more precarious than that?" Thus, the ruler of the state of Jin realized his misdeeds and gave an order to halt construction. From then on, "as precarious as a stack of eggs," came to apply to a dangerous situation. "*

I love these colorful stories. Idioms like this are one of the reasons why watching a foreign movie, while enjoyable, may seem incomprehensible at times. There is a vast amount of cultural reference that we are missing as outsiders, which leaves us unable to reference many of the events and colorful touches that the movie contains.

Maintaining a complex information networking environment can be very tricky. There may be many, many different elements involved, from the workstations and servers, to the switches, routers, firewalls and other devices. Unless the environment has been architected well, a single flaw can leave the network completely vulnerable. Thus, despite having a wide array of tools and solutions in place, the network security may yet be "as precarious as a stack of eggs."

Security flaws can have a cascading effect[35]. However, even a perfectly engineered network can still fall victim to a zero-day (or 0-day) attack[36]. Thus, we must be vigilant about proper maintenance and patching of equipment, as well as testing for the proper segmentation of risks.

Similarly, I can see this applying to project management. Sometimes projects may run long, and not through any fault of those involved. Rushing a critical, sensitive project may lead to disaster.

## To gain the initiative by striking first[37]

(先發制人 Xiān Fā Zhì Rén)

*"In 209 BC, open revolts against the Qin Dynasty were raging all across China[38]. The magistrate of Guji went to see Xiang Liang (a rebel leader) and said, "He who strikes first will gain the initiative, while he who delays will be subjugated. So, I have come to ask you to*

---

[35] See *Core Software Security: Security at the Source* by James Ransome, pg. 218, or *International Guide to Cyber Security* by Jody R. Westby, pg. 26

[36] A zero-day vulnerability refers to a hole in software that is unknown to the vendor. This security hole is then exploited by hackers before the vendor becomes aware and hurries to fix it—this exploit is called a zero-day attack.

[37] *The Stories Behind 100 Chinese Idioms, Sinolingua, 1998, pg. 78*

[38] See *Dynastic China: An Elementary History* by Tan Koon San, pg. 70

*join me in revolt at once." Xiang Liang pretended to agree. He then convinced his nephew Xiang Yu to slay the magistrate and his followers, numbering over one hundred men. Thus, the people of Guji flocked to Xiang Liang and followed him in the struggle to topple the Qin Dynasty. Later, "to gain the initiative by striking first" came to mean that he who acts first will succeed in subduing others."*

When looking to the defense of a network, and a business' critical data infrastructure, we are not typically afforded the luxury of knowing when an enemy actor will attack us. Because of this, it is critical to run regular penetration testing[39] against your network. We can gain the initiative here, by striking first against ourselves, finding the flaws, and fixing them, all long before our enemy has the opportunity to try it himself. Penetration testing does not guarantee that all flaws will be detected, but it is about the best can hope for, and it is the closest thing to simulating a real attack.

Another possible interpretation here, although far less common in practice, would be to 'hack the hacker.' Sometimes, we may become aware of an attempted attack by the first tentative probes from a malicious actor. A good hacker is always attempting to be subtle enough not to set off any alarms that might alert his intended victim(s). There have been some very fascinating stories about an

---

[39] A penetration test, or pentest, is an attempt to evaluate the security of an IT infrastructure by safely trying to exploit vulnerabilities. These vulnerabilities may exist in operating systems, service and application flaws, hardware, improper configurations, or risky end-user behavior.

incident responder detecting the hacker, and in fact, managing to gain access to the hacker's systems[40]! By striking first and directly, we can certainly gain the initiative, and possibly foil not only the attempt against us, but other intended targets as well. Please be aware of local laws where applicable, as this may not be legal in your area.

## Repairing the road while making a secret detour[41]
(明修栈道，暗渡陳倉  Míng Xiū Zhàn Dào Àn Dù Chén Cāng)

*"In 205 BC, Liu Bang was crowned king of Han, and became the first emperor of the Han Dynasty. However, because the military strength of his arch-rival, Xiang Yu, was much stronger, Liu Bang was forced to retreat with his 30,000 men to his stronghold of Hanzhong. This area was surrounded by mountains, and the main way to approach it was along a plank road built along the face of a cliff. Liu Bang burned the plank road as soon as his men were safely past it to show Xiang Yu that he had no intention of returning, and to prevent a possible pursuit. After about half a year, Liu Bang sent men to rebuild the*

---

[40] See http://www.techrepublic.com/article/hacking-the-hacker-how-a-consultant-shut-down-a-malicious-user/ or http://www.forbes.com/sites/marcwebertobias/2012/04/26/hacking-the-hackers-a-counter-intelligence-operation-against-digital-gangs/

[41] *The Stories Behind 100 Chinese Idioms, Sinolingua, 1998, pg.105*

*road. Naturally, Xiang Yu thought that meant that an attack was being prepared along that route, and that it would not be forthcoming until the road had been made serviceable again. Meanwhile, Liu Bang secretly led a force into Guanzhong by way of the perilous Chancang Pass and caught Xiang Lu by surprise. From then on, Liu Bang began to contend with Xiang Lu for the central parts of China. Later, "repairing the road while making a secret detour" came to be used to describe and obvious action that is camouflage for a devious stratagem."*

This sounds like a perfect analogy for a honeypot to me. Honeypot Systems are decoy servers or systems setup to gather information regarding an attacker or intruder into your system. It is important to remember that Honeypots should replace other traditional Internet security systems. They should be used as an additional level or system[42] to protect a network. With a honeypot in place, an attacker sees an obvious, and tempting, vulnerable system, perhaps under the guise of a system being built or repaired. However, the honeypot (properly) is totally separated from any other systems[43]. Once the attacker has been lured into the honeypot, much can be learned about the attempted attack, and attacker. In fact, this might even lead to the opportunity I wrote about in the previous section, regarding 'hacking the hacker.' The knowledge gained from

---

[42] See https://www.sans.org/security-resources/idfaq/what-is-a-honeypot/1/9

[43] This is an advanced technique, and is absolutely not advised, unless it is being managed by an experienced Information Security engineer.

monitoring honeypot systems can give us advanced warning about new offensive techniques being employed, and can lead to new threat signatures, and point to previously undiscovered vulnerabilities.

## You must enter the tiger's den to catch his cubs[44]

**(不入虎穴, 焉得虎子 Bù Rù Hǔ Xué,Yān De Hǔ Zi)**

*"When Ban Chao was an envoy to the Western Region, he once went to visit the King of Shanshan[45], with a small entourage of only 36 men. The king treated him with the utmost hospitality, until an envoy from the Xiongnu[46] arrived with a large retinue, which caused the king to suddenly give Ban Chao the cold shoulder. Realizing that both his mission and his life were in danger, Ban Chao devised a desperate plan: he would launch a surprise attack on the Xiongnu encampment at night, beating gongs and setting fire to the tents. When the Xiongnu rushed out in a panic, his people would slay them. When his men express alarm at such a perilous undertaking, Ban Chao said, "How can you catch tiger cubs without first entering the tiger's den?"*

---

[44] *The Stories Behind 100 Chinese Idioms, Sinolingua, 1998, pg.187*

[45] About 73 AD, see *Imperial Chinese Military History: 8000 BC-1912 AD* by Marvin C. Whiting, pg. 194.

[46] A nomadic, proto-Mongol ethnic group. See *The Silk Road: Two Thousand Years in the Heart of Asia,* by Frances Wood, pg. 48

*So, they carried out the plan, and annihilated the Xiongnu's tents, thereby winning the King of Shanshan's allegiance to the Han emperor. Later, the saying "you must enter the tiger's den to catch his cubs" came to mean that no great enterprise can be successful without some risk being taken."*

This sounds like a Red Team[47] tactic to me. A Red Team or hacker might find a situation where it makes sense to deliberately cause a noisy attack against a certain part of a company, in order to draw attention away from another area. For example, the attackers might choose to execute a Christmas Attack[48] against a web server, and while the incident response team is scrambling to analyze and

---

[47] A Red Team is an internal, or contracted, group that carries out simulated attacks against an organization. This is similar to penetration testing. Contrast this with a Blue Team, which is tasked with handling incident response.

[48] See *Aries Security Essentials,* 2.1.4: "A Christmas tree attack sends a large number of Christmas tree packets to an end device. A Christmas tree packet has all the options set so that any protocol can be used. The name is derived from the idea that all the settings are turned to "on" within the packet so it is lit up like a Christmas tree.

Christmas tree packets require much more processing by routers and end devices than other packets. Large numbers of these packets can use up so much processing power that it ties up these devices effectively making any other task nearly impossible thus denying service to legitimate traffic. Receiving these types of packets is not usual and therefore should be regarded as suspicious. Intrusion detection systems can detect these packets as do some firewalls.

prevent the attack, the hacker attacks his true target: the HVAC[49] system. Alternatively, a hacker might leak false press releases about a company of a horrible nature. While the company struggles to contain the PR mess in a full-fledged panic, the hacker can infiltrate various systems freely. This is also the perfect time to do a little Social Engineering.

Social engineering, in the context of information security, refers to the psychological manipulation of people into performing actions or divulging confidential information. A type of confidence trick for the purpose of information gathering, fraud, or system access, it differs from a traditional "con" in that it is often one of many steps in a more complex fraud scheme.

For more information on diversion and misdirection with regards to information security, see *"The Hacker Ethos: The Beginner's Guide to Ethical Hacking and Penetration Testing"* by True Demon.


## 3. On Military Matters (De Rei Militari)


Publius Flavius Vegetius Renatus was a Roman from the 4th century. He wrote De Rei Miltari in 390 A.D., and we have an

---

[49] Heating, ventilation and air conditioning systems, often networked in the modern enterprise.

excellent English translation available to us by one Lieutenant John Clarke in 1767. In his Memoirs, Montecuculli, the conqueror of the Turks at St. Gotthard, wrote: "*However, there are spirits bold enough to believe themselves great captains as soon as they know how to handle a horse, carry a lance at charge in a tournament, or as soon as they have read the precepts of Vegetius.*" Such was the reputation of Vegetius for a thousand years[50]. This is a wonderful source extant to us from ancient Rome. Vegetius himself mentions a work now lost to us from Cato the Elder, called *De Re Militari*, as well. Such a shame!

All of the sections quoted here are from Book III.


## Preface to Book III


*"He, therefore, who desires peace, should prepare for war. He who aspires to victory, should spare no pains to form his soldiers. And he who hopes for success, should fight on principle, not chance. No one dares to offend or insult a power of known superiority in action."*

[Igitur qui desiderat pacem, praeparet bellum; qui uictoriam cupit, milites inbuat diligenter; qui secundos optat euentus, dimicet arte, non

---

[50] *Roots of Strategy*, by Thomas R. Phillips

casu. Nemo prouocare, nemo audet offendere quem intellegit superiorem esse, si pugnet.]

Commonly paraphrased as *"Si vis pacem, para bellum"* or, "If you want peace, prepare for war," Publius echos concepts in Greek and Roman thought as far back as Plato in his Νόμοι (Laws)[51].

It is not enough to build an environment according to best practices, or compliance requirements – we must prepare for digital battle. It is not if a business will be compromised, but when. In fact, a survey done back in 2015 showed that 80-85% of businesses self-reported that they had been hacked or compromised in some way already[52]. Therefore, we must both design our systems from the ground up, assuming that they will be under continual threat of attack, and train our staff in various methods to be able to hunt, identify, and disrupt such attacks. Defense is simply not enough. There is a saying in Information Security: "prevention is ideal, but detection is a must."

A side note – where one might assume that Publius speaks from hubris in his last line, he is actually being very specific. If it is well known that an opponent has superior technology in warfare (i.e.,

---

[51] Plato, Laws, 1.628c9–e1.

[52] https://www.cfosurvey.org/press-release/more-than-80-percent-of-firms-say-they-have-been-hacked/

they have tanks, we have sticks), then no one would dare attack them.

Additionally, we have a great maxim here about training. If you truly want to have the best possible hope of a secure network, make sure your team gets the best possible training. This is not an area to be a spendthrift. With a field as large and complex as information security, it is woefully common to find professionals in their field that simply do not know what they do not know.

In the field of psychology, the Dunning–Kruger effect is a cognitive bias in which people mistakenly assess their cognitive ability as greater than it is. It is related to the cognitive bias of illusory superiority and it comes from the inability of people to recognize their lack of ability. Without the self-awareness of metacognition, people cannot objectively evaluate their competence or incompetence.

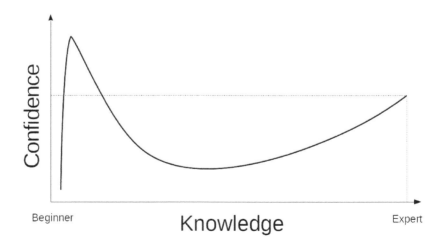

Without training and experience over time, that initial spike in one's confidence may last for a long time. This can lead to devastating gaps in knowledge and ability. This, of course, leads to significant holes in our defenses by those who do not realize there are major areas of concern that they are ignorant of.

## Section 1 – There is Weakness in Complexity:

*"An army too numerous is subject to many dangers and inconveniences. Its bulk makes it slow and unwieldy in its motions; and as it is obliged to march in columns of great length, it is exposed to the risk of being continually harassed and insulted by inconsiderable parties of the enemy."*

[Nam pluribus casibus subiacet amplior multitudo; in itineribus pro mole sua semper est tardior, in longiore autem agmine etiam a paucis superuentum adsolet pati.]

Several applications arise from this. First, that monitoring and maintaining a network certainly becomes more and more difficult as the number of nodes, endpoints, and other resources increase. How does one keep any semblance of control over a network or networks, as they scale to hundreds, or thousands of devices? Vegetius goes into great detail about the order and segmentation of the Roman Army. *In similo modo,* we must segment our networks as they grow, and maintain ranks of engineers who are responsible for their segment, with various levels of oversight as needed. For example, a corporation may have 10,000 computers, and varying numbers of affiliated networking hardware and other networked devices. It is most common to first divide a network geographically, that is, by building, campus, or city. Depending on the size, it may be further necessary to divide by department or function, as these units typically have differing security needs and resources. So, we divide the network into accounting, call center, administration, manufacturing, etc. Network Administrators can be placed at any or all of these levels as needed, with clear hierarchy and reporting policies. All of these report to the 'General', that is, the Chief Information Officer, Chief Technology Officer, or perhaps the more recent C-level position, the Chief Information Security Officer (CISO).

Secondly, the sheer complexity of an organization may lead to its downfall. Even with proper organization of its administrators, a network that has too many different devices from many different vendors presents its own challenges. It becomes increasingly difficult to monitor and maintain devices, as the number of brands and vendors increase. Each one will have its own flaws, vulnerabilities, and required configurations. Centralized management tools help, as do network device monitoring tools, but when trying to scale, automation is key, and it becomes increasingly difficult to automate when you have to script or code for numerous different devices. Even if implementing a System Information and Event Monitoring solution (SIEM), there will be so much noise from so many different formats, that it may become impossible to sort through. While it is true that most businesses grow their infrastructure organically, that is, here and there as they need it and opportunity arises, at some point, one must carefully architect the entire network, and standardize on certain vendors.

## Section 3 – Famine Leads to Desperation:

*"Famine makes greater havoc in an army than the enemy, and is more terrible than the sword. Time and opportunity may help to retrieve other misfortunes, but where forage and provisions have not been carefully provided, the evil is without remedy. The main and principal point in war is to secure plenty of provisions and to destroy the enemy by famine."*

[Ordo postulat, ut de commeatu pabulo frumentisque dicatur. Saepius enim penuria quam pugna consumit exercitum, et ferro saeuior fames est. Deinde reliquis casibus potest in tempore subueniri, pabulatio et annona in necessitate remedium non habent, nisi ante condantur. In omni expeditione unum est et maximum telum, ut tibi sufficiat uictus, hostes frangat inopia.]

Vegetius says multiple times throughout his work that a general that can win by starving an enemy, rather than engage in open warfare, is a far greater general. There are modern attacks against which we must defend, and we can learn about this here. The first is that of the Distributed Denial of Service attack, or DDoS. This is an attack in which multiple compromised computer systems attack a target, such as a server, website or other network resource, and cause it to be unusable for users of the targeted resource. The flood of incoming messages, data, connection requests or malformed packets to the target system will force it to slow down or even crash and shut down or reboot, thereby denying service to legitimate users or systems. In this way, by blocking the flow of access to these resources, the users become 'starved' of their data or internet access.

These attacks are very difficult to defend against. Filtering the bad data may not work, as it will simply overload the firewalls. One can purchase and deploy dedicated DDoS mitigation appliances, which are specialized hardware that sits in an enterprise's data center in front of the normal servers and routers and are specifically built to detect and filter the malicious traffic. However, they are very expensive, and may sit around and do nothing until you get attacked. Even then, they may still buckle under the weight of a large attack.

If a single network or network device is being attacked, it may be possible to utilize a secondary internet connection to allow the intended traffic, both incoming and outgoing. However, this is a temporary measure, and would still require some modification of network devices to implement during an attack. Only if the attackers are focusing on a specific IP Address[53], rather than a domain name, will this form of defense then be successful.

---

[53] A unique string of numbers separated by periods that identifies each computer using the Internet Protocol to communicate over a network.

For protecting websites, one can use cloud services which can provide temporary mitigation and buffering. In this case, all attack traffic that would otherwise directly hit your server is automatically routed through the service's distributed network of data centers. Once the attack traffic is shifted, they are able to leverage their very large network and infrastructure to absorb the floods of attack traffic at their network edge, and only forward the 'good' data traffic to your servers.

As Vegetius says later: *"famine, according to the common proverb, is an internal enemy that makes more havoc than the sword."*

Thus, to avoid being starved, either have sufficient resources in advance, or have alternate means of getting them during an attack.

## Section 6 – Social Engineering Attacks the Weakest Link:

*"Our spies should be constantly abroad; we should spare no pains in tampering with their men, and give all manner of encouragement to deserters. By these means we may get intelligence of their present or future designs."*

[Vt nostra commoditas est sapienter ista uitare, ita, si aduersariorum imperitia uel dissimulatio occasionem nobis dederit, non oportet omitti, sed explorare sollicite, proditores ac transfugas inuitare, ut, quid hostis moliatur in praesenti uel in futurum, possimus agnoscere.]

The wise adversary understands this: that despite millions of dollars of hardware, software, and physical security in place, the weakest link is always the user. This is why Social Engineering attacks work so well[54].

Kevin Mitnick, one of the world's most famous hackers from the early days of the internet, once said *"People are prone to taking mental shortcuts. They may know that they shouldn't give out certain information, but the fear of not being nice, the fear of appearing ignorant, the fear of a perceived authority figure - all these are triggers, which can be used by a social engineer to convince a person to override established security procedures."*

The people behind the machines may be as much a risk as those attackers from outside. All staff must be properly vetted, trained, and continually educated on IT security best practices and basic common-sense concepts. Training is cheap and easy with web-based video training. There really should be very few times when a person is successfully duped into clicking a false link, giving a password to a stranger over the phone, or opening an odd email attachment. Yet, this continues to happen regularly. How much more difficult is it to mitigate when one of the users is successfully convinced to assist an

---

[54] Social engineering here might be using deception, manipulation and influence to convince a human who has access to a computer system to do something, like click on an attachment in an e-mail.

outside agent? We can implement some protections, but they are limited in the scope of their defense.

If we properly silo access to data based on various access controls, we can at least contain the damage. In Information Security, we have many types of access controls:

1. **Attribute-based Access Control (ABAC)**

   An access control paradigm whereby access rights are granted to users through the use of policies which evaluate attributes (user attributes, resource attributes and environment conditions)

2. **Discretionary Access Control (DAC)**

   In DAC, the data owner determines who can access specific resources. For example, a system administrator may create a hierarchy of files to be accessed based on certain permissions.

3. **History-Based Access Control (HBAC)**

   Access is granted or declined based on the real-time evaluation of a history of activities of the inquiring party, e.g. behavior, time between requests, content of requests. For example, the access to a certain service or data source can be granted or declined on the personal behavior, e.g. the request interval exceeds one query per second.

4. **Identity-Based Access Control (IBAC)**

   Using IBAC, network administrators can more effectively manage activity and access based on individual needs.

5. **Mandatory Access Control (MAC)**

   In MAC, users do not have much freedom to determine who has access to their files. For example, security clearance of users and classification of data (as confidential, secret or top secret) are used as security labels to define the level of trust.

6. **Organization-Based Access control (OrBAC)**

   The OrBAC model allows the policy designer to define a security policy independently of the implementation.

7. **Role-Based Access Control (RBAC)**

   RBAC allows access based on the job title. RBAC largely eliminates discretion when providing access to objects. For example, a human resources specialist should not have permissions to create network accounts; this should be a role reserved for network administrators.

8. **Rule-Based Access Control (RAC)**

   The RAC method is largely context based. An example of this would be only allowing students to use the labs during a certain time of day.

9. **Responsibility Based Access Control**

   Information is accessed based on the responsibilities
   assigned to an actor or a business role[55].

Additionally, we can attempt to detect if a user is suddenly doing
things they ought not to be doing, by means of anomaly detection
software that flags abnormal user activity. It can be very difficult to
detect this anomalous user behavior, although there are solutions
available that claim be effective.


Section 8 – Reconnaissance and Research is Power:

*"It is essential to know the character of the enemy and of their
principal officers - whether they be. rash or cautious, enterprising or
timid, whether they fight on principle or from chance and whether
the nations they have been engaged with were brave or cowardly."*

[Ad rem pertinet, qualis ipse aduersarius uel eius comites
optimatesque sint, nosse, utrum temerarii an cauti, audaces an
timidi, scientes artem bellicam uel ex usu an temere pugnantes; quae
gentes cum his fortes, quae ignauae sint.]

It may in fact be useful to a potential attacker, who is still in his
research phase, to sift through publicly available information. Such
as, hiring notices, press releases, and resumes online to find out

---

[55] See https://en.wikipedia.org/wiki/Access_control

about the actual people in various security roles[56]. From this information, much and more can be learned about how much experience the person in charge of data security has.

For example, a public DNS entry may point to "antivirusvendor.domain.com". using this information, an attacker may be able to develop a targeted exploit to bypass their endpoint protection software vendor. Or, an industry publication may laud the enterprise on their innovative or cost-saving solution that was just implemented by Vendor X. Just as above, a custom attack may be devised.

It is important to limit what information is given out publicly, where possible, on these matters. Knowing their vendor certifications can lead to a knowledge of what possible defenses and equipment are in place, while finding these users on social media can leak tantalizing tidbits of information, such as when they go on vacation, what their vices are, and what their personality type is. All this information can be used in conjunction with social engineering hacks, or. At the very least, knowing how the person might react to a certain kind of attack.

## Section 18 – Be Sudden and Random:

*"You must always endeavor to get the start of your enemy in drawing up in order of battle, as you will then have it in your power to make*

---

[56] AKA OSINT

*your proper dispositions without obstruction. This will increase the
courage of your own troops and intimidate your adversaries. For a
superiority of courage seems to be implied on the side of an army
that offers battle, whereas troops begin to be fearful who see their
enemies ready to attack them. You will also secure another great
advantage, that of marching up in order and falling upon them while
forming and still in confusion. For part of the victory consists in
throwing the enemy into disorder before you engage them."*

[Semper autem studere debes, ut prior instruas aciem, quia ex
arbitrio tuo potes facere quod tibi utile iudicas, cum nullus obsistit;
deinde et tuis auges confidentiam et aduersariis fiduciam minuis,
quia fortiores uidentur qui prouocare non dubitant. Inimici autem
incipiunt formidare, qui uident contra se acies ordinari. Hinc additur
maximum commodum, quia tu instructus paratusque ordinantem et
trepidum aduersarium praeoccupas. Pars enim uictoriae est
inimicum turbare, antequam dimices.]

The last line is the most applicable here and harkens to my previous
commentary on diversion and misdirection. Yet also, time is always
of the essence when attempting to infiltrate a network. When flaws
are discovered, and vulnerabilities are leaked, one must attack
quickly if he wants to breach before it is patched. There can be
considerable lead time between a vulnerability disclosure, and the
time it takes for a patch to be developed, pushed to clients, and
implemented. The attacker knows this and may strike fast, and hard.
A careful balance must be sought here. If a network engineer always

patches systems the instant the patch comes out, disaster may still strike. It is not uncommon for a patch to have its own vulnerabilities, possibly even worse than before. It is also possible that the patch may not be properly and fully tested, resulting in crashes and other failures. There is no perfect answer here, however, there are good sources for systems administrators to utilize of other groups of users who have beta tested[57] the patches. It is also a best practice to deploy new patches in a test environment first, before deploying to production equipment and systems.

## Section 26 – Obfuscate to Frustrate:

*"On finding the enemy has notice of your designs, you must immediately alter your plan of operations. Consult with many on proper measures to be taken, but communicate the plans you intend to put in execution to few, and those only of the most assured fidelity; or rather trust no one but yourself."*

[Cum consilium tuum cognoueris aduersariis proditum, dispositionem mutare te conuenit. Quid fieri debeat, tractato cum

---

[57] In software development, a beta test is the second phase of software testing in which a sampling of the intended audience tries the product out. Beta is the second letter of the Greek alphabet. Originally, the term alpha test meant the first phase of testing in a software development process, and is still sometimes used.

multis, quid uero facturus sis, cum paucissimis ac fidelissimis uel potius ipse tecum.]

Again, we must be cautious about what sort of information is released to the public. A large organization, enterprise or government agency may release an RFP[58] or RFQ[59]. Inside those requests is a plethora of information, in great detail about exactly what sort of equipment, from which vendors, is going to be installed. An attacker can utilize that information to plan his vulnerability probing and attacks. If it is legally possible, it may be wise to remove this information after the projects are completed, obfuscate it, or create documents with false information, to lead attackers astray. However, this is likely not possible for governmental or publicly traded entities. At least, perhaps the information can be archived after some time, or paced behind some kind of a form request, so we make the hacker work a bit harder to get at it. Internally, some organizations may choose to have false DNS entries or falsely open ports and active IPs to slow the attacker. Ultimately, there is not much to be done to mitigate this, but we should still be aware of it.

---

[58] A request for proposal (RFP) is a document that solicits proposals, often made through a bidding process, by an agency or company interested in procurement of a commodity, service or valuable asset, to potential suppliers to submit business proposals.

[59] A request for quotation (RFQ) is a standard business process whose purpose is to invite suppliers into a bidding process to bid on specific products or services. RFQ generally means the same thing as IFB (Invitation For Bid).

# 4. Sun Tzu – The Art of War

Possibly the best-known author in this book, Master Sun Wu of China, (also known to us as Sun Tzu, or 孙子) wrote this classic treatise during the Warring States period[60]. His knowledge has been appreciated by rulers, generals, businessmen and scholars for almost 2,500 years. Truly, this was one of the first books that came to mind when I decided to compile this work. Vast amounts of material have been written by many authors far more capable than I on Master Sun and his strategies, so I shall give him very little introduction here. Due to the culturally accepted habits of ascribing works to famous persons, and peering through the murky lenses of time, we may never determine if this book was written by only one man, and if it was the historical figure of Sun Wu. However, let that not interfere with the wisdom contain therein, nor let it cloud the possibilities of its modern applications.

## Book I – Laying Plans (計篇第一)

*"All warfare is based on deception.*

---

[60] About 403-221 B.C.

*Hence, when able to attack, we must seem unable; when using our forces, we must seem inactive; when we are near, we must make the enemy believe we are far away; when far away, we must make him believe we are near.*

*Hold out baits to entice the enemy. Feign disorder, and crush him[61]."*

[兵者, 龍道也。

故能而示之不能, 用而示之不用, 近而示之遠, 遠而 示之近。

利而誘之, 亂而取之。]

Security researchers realized some time ago, that if you set up a truly tempting target, there is a good chance that someone will take the bait. In an earlier chapter, I spoke about honeypots, and this text seems like as clear a call to use them as anything. Honeypots are not simply useful for learning about who is trying to hack you, but they can also be helpful to lead an attacker into wasting his time and efforts on a harmless, segregated system.

What other forms of deception are useful in IT Security? There are enough methods that the famous early hacker Kevin Mitnick wrote a book called *"The Art of Deception."* We use deception regularly to obfuscate code in web apps. It's used in Social Engineering constantly. It's used by malware authors to evade detection from

---

[61] Book I, Lines 18-20

users and antivirus alike (using false file and process names). As a response, antivirus and anti-malware programs use deception in order to avoid being disabled by malicious code (using the same techniques as above).

Attackers may also use deceptive techniques such as using proxy servers to hide their true origin, or even leaving behind false clues in order to implicate another group. For example, When North Korean hackers breached Sony Pictures in 2014 to prevent the release of the Kim Jong-un assassination comedy The Interview, for instance, they invented a hacktivist group called Guardians of Peace and tried to throw off investigators with a vague demand for "monetary compensation." Even after the FBI officially named North Korea as the culprit and the White House imposed new sanctions against the Kim regime as punishment, several security firms continued to argue that the attack must have been an inside job, a story picked up by numerous news outlets—including WIRED.


When state-sponsored Russian hackers stole and leaked emails from the Democratic National Committee and Hillary Clinton's campaign in 2016, we now know that the Kremlin likewise created diversions and cover stories. It invented a lone Romanian hacker named Guccifer 2.0 to take credit for the hacks; it also spread the rumors that a murdered DNC staffer named Seth Rich had leaked the emails from inside the organization—and it distributed many of the stolen documents through a fake whistle-blowing site called DCLeaks. Those deceptions became conspiracy theories[62]. The public then picks up on these deceptions and amplifies it, causing additional challenges with response.

## Book II – Waging War (作戰篇第二)

*"When you engage in actual fighting, if victory is long in coming, the men's weapons will grow dull and their ardor will be damped. If you lay siege to a town, you will exhaust your strength.*

*Again, if the campaign is protracted, the resources of the State will not be equal to the strain[63]."*

[其用戰也勝久則純兵挫銳, 攻城則力屈。

久暴師則國用不足。]

Could this be another example of a DDoS attack? With a long enough attack, an organization may be faced with either paying up and hoping the attack stops or potentially going out of business. Yet this also works both ways. If a network is able to thwart its attacker for long enough, the attacker may give up. Unless an attack is highly

---

[62] https://www.wired.com/story/untold-story-2018-olympics-destroyer-cyberattack/
[63] Book II, Lines 2-3

targeted, many hackers are more interested in the low hanging fruit, and don't want to tie up their own resources for long.

I believe the converse of this is true as well, focusing on peacetime. Without red team/blue team exercises and regular simulations, the staff that is tasked with securing the enterprise network may become complacent, and their skills will begin to diminish. Tabletop exercises and Incident Response training are critical to keeping the weapons of the response team sharp. Similarly, attackers and Red Team members in training may participate in CTF exercises. CTFs or "Capture the Flag" events are hacking games where a person or team is required to retrieve a 'flag' that is usually a string of text. The flags become increasingly difficult as the game progresses and requires strong skills from many various disciplines.

## Book III - Attack by Stratagem (謀攻篇第三)

*"There are three ways in which a ruler can bring misfortune upon his army: (1) By commanding the army to advance or to retreat, being ignorant of the fact that it cannot obey. This is called hobbling the army. (2) By attempting to govern an army in the same way as he administers a kingdom, being ignorant of the conditions that obtain in an army. This causes restlessness in the soldier's mind. (3) By employing the officers of this army without discrimination, through*

*ignorance of the military principle of adaptation to circumstances. This shakes the confidence of the soldiers."*

[故君之所以患于軍者三： 不知軍之不以進而謂之進, 不知軍之不以退而 謂之退, 是為魔軍; 不知三軍之事, 而同三軍之政者, 則軍士惑矣; 不知三軍之權, 而同三軍之任, 則軍士疑矣。]


One area we have not spoken of much yet, is the actual methods of managing one's security team. In smaller organizations, this might only be one person. However, in an enterprise environment, this might be a CIO or CTO, a CISO[64], and various levels of management, all the way down to the actual technicians and engineers. Too often, orders may come down from on high; executive decisions being made without a deep enough understanding of the technology and risks involved. There needs to be a clear and reasonable flow of information in both directions. If the engineers feel that their concerns are being ignored, or that they are being given tasks that make no sense to them, they will certainly grow as restless as the army troops that Master Sun refers to. Additionally, there must be enough trust in the skills of the team, along with quality, continually evaluated and revised, processes in place. When that is lacking,

---

[64] Chief Information Security Officer, a position that is starting to see some traction in the Enterprise.

micromanagement tends to set in. in that sort of environment, it is very easy to lose excellent staff.

Technology and Information Security concerns are not static, and require continuous training to be relevant and successful, but also knowledge of human behavior and effective management techniques.

*"If you know the other and know yourself, you can have 100 battles without danger. If you do not know the other, but know yourself, you will have one win and one loss. If you do not know the other and do not know yourself, every battle will be lost."*

[知彼知己，百戰不殆；不知彼而知己，一勝一負；不知彼，不知己，每戰必殆]

If an organization truly knows itself, its contents and its structure, attacks are much more easy to detect and prevent. This is why many Cybersecurity Frameworks begin with a proper inventory of all assets, both physical and digital. Once an inventory has been completed, a proper baseline can begin. We must know as nearly exactly as possible what expected performance and behavior looks like for our organization. Suddenly seeing a spike in network traffic, or a sustained burst of CPU usage on a server can be significant indicators of compromise. If we know every single file that belongs on our web server, and have the verified correct hashes of them, the new can instantly detect if a file has been altered maliciously.

This is still not commonly done and is a major reason why some breaches can last for months, or even years without detection. Major organizations are losing battles they did not even realize they were fighting.

## Book IV - Tactical Dispositions (形篇第四)

*"To secure ourselves against defeat lies in our own hands, but the opportunity of defeating the enemy is provided by the enemy himself."*

[不勝在己, 勝在敵。]

I love how concise the Chinese script is here. Just seven characters gives us that whole sentence in English. All too often, we are our own worst enemies, whether we realize it or not. Between falling for Social Engineering, fatigue, forgetting follow a policy, or simply making a bad decision, and despite a large budget, and the best tools available, sometimes we leave the door wide open to our foes. This is one of the reasons that having rock solid policies and procedures in place can greatly mitigate these risks. All Standard Operating Procedures (SOPs) need to be continually revised, as technology and times change. By incorporating Quality Assurance checks to catch missed steps and errors, the vast majority of tasks can be made to be consistent, with repeated, desirable results. This is not to say the quality SOPs will prevent any errors from happening, and they themselves may cause their own errors, but they are the best way to ensure task results, especially when trying to scale. It may seem onerous as a small business, but as the company grows, the procedural documentation and standards will be invaluable, especially when training a new staff member.

I also see this a as a call to continuingly study the latest threats and risk studies. In the ivory towers of the enterprise, it is possible to lose the connection with the field. The engineers and the front-line folks who see what sort of attacks are trending to occur have valuable insight as to what sort of defenses need be deployed. We must not always trust the reports and fancy presentations coming from our vendors. Additionally, continuing education from quality sources such as SANS[65] and CompTIA[66] will help greatly with this.

## Book V – Energy (執篇第五]

*"In all fighting, the direct method may be used for joining battle, but indirect methods will be needed in order to secure victory.*

---

[65] The SANS Institute (officially the Escal Institute of Advanced Technologies) is a private U.S. for-profit company founded in 1989 that specializes in information security, cybersecurity training and selling certificates. Topics available for training include cyber and network defenses, penetration testing, incident response, digital forensics, and audit. The information security courses are developed through a consensus process involving administrators, security managers, and information security professionals. The courses cover security fundamentals and technical aspects of information security. The Institute has been recognized for its training programs and certification programs. SANS stands for SysAdmin, Audit, Network and Security.

[66] The Computing Technology Industry Association (CompTIA), a non-profit trade association, issuing professional certifications for the information technology (IT) industry. It is considered one of the IT industry's top trade associations. Based in Downers Grove, Illinois, CompTIA issues vendor-neutral professional certification in over 120 countries. The organization releases over 50 industry studies annually to track industry trends and changes.

*The direct and the indirect lead on to each other in turn. It is like moving in a circle—you never come to an end. Who can exhaust the possibilities of their combination?"*

[凡戰者, 以正合, 以奇勝.

奇正相生, 如循環之無端, 孰能窮之. ]


When performing Red Team exercises, it is sometimes useful to attack full force, to see how well the defenses hold up. However, there are great reasons for a subtler approach, as well. If the firewall is being lit up with alerts, one would hope that the admins are well aware that an attack is happening. What we want is for the team to be aware that an attack is happening, even when there is very little indication of such. During a real-world attack, we may only see the slightest of signs. In order to perform a less obvious penetration test, here are some things the tester can do:

1. Extend the delays between port scans, pings, and other active requests.
2. Break up the requests into small groups.
3. Test attacks in a lab environment before hammering away at a production system. Once the tester is more experienced, he can accomplish more with less.
4. If a vulnerability that can be exploited is found, the tester can try to use it on a different system than the one that was scanned.

5. This may not be practical for Red Team exercises, but a real hacker might be willing to play a very long game – waiting weeks or months after finding a hole to attack.

As I have said before, technology is not a static thing, and thus the training and exercises must continue in turns, indefinitely.

## Book VI - Weak Points and Strong (虛實篇第六)

*"You can be sure of succeeding in your attack if you only attack places that are undefended. You can ensure the safety of your defense if you only hold positions that cannot be attacked.*

*Hence that general is skillful in attack whose opponent does not know what to defend, and he is skillful in defense whose opponent does not know what to attack."*

[攻而必取者, 攻其所不守也。守而必固者, 守其所 不攻也。

故善攻者, 敵不知其所守。善守者, 敵不知其所攻。]

Proper reconnaissance is critical before choosing your target. According to the EC-Council's Certified Ethical Hacker (CEH) material, successful black hat operations will typically follow five phases: Reconnaissance, Scanning, Gaining Access, Maintaining Access, and Covering Tracks. Reconnaissance is probably the longest phase, sometimes lasting weeks or months.  The black hat or penetration tester uses a variety of sources to learn as much as possible about the target business. By ensuring that the target to be attacked is truly vulnerable before launching exploits, the hacker can know that they can slip into the system while making as little noise as possible.

This also touches on the point regarding system complexity being difficult to protect. More importantly, it raises the opposite point: one can make a system more complex to make it more difficult to hack.

There are 1023 standard defined system ports[67], although one can choose any of 65,536 possible ports to use. By changing the port for a standard service, such as FTP, and administrator can make the system more difficult to be hacked. There are intelligent port scanning tools that can still determine where an FTP server is located, but forcing the attacker to scan thousands of ports to find it makes the attacker's job much noisier to complete. Similarly, renaming standard system accounts such as root or Administrator can also break a lot of hacks, viruses, and scripts.

Book VIII – Variation of Tactics (九變篇第八)

---

[67] https://www.iana.org/assignments/service-names-port-numbers/service-names-port-numbers.xhtml

*"There are five dangerous faults that may affect a general: (1) Recklessness, which leads to destruction; (2) cowardice, which leads to capture; (3) a nasty temper, which can be provoked by insults; (4) a delicacy of honor that is sensitive to shame; (5) over solicitude for his men, which exposes him to worry and trouble."*

[故將有五危:必死, 殺也;必生, 虞也;忿速, 侮 也;廉潔, 辱也;愛民, 煩也。]

Ultimately, it is the people that power the technology. It is of critical importance that the system administrator, and those in charge of defending our networks and data, do not become complacent. All too often, arrogance and hubris have led to data breaches, where an admin that accepts advice and regular discourse on the best courses of action, will have a far better chance at protection. The Information Technology industry as a whole tends to have had a history of engineers with issues socializing. There seems to be some scientific basis for this, in fact[68]. While I do not seek here to provide social advice, it seems that it is just as important to regularly receive peer feedback about interpersonal communications as it is to perform regular vulnerability assessments on networks.

Non-traditional management and personal skills, such as emotional intelligence, proper boundaries, receiving therapy, and

---

[68] https://www.timeshighereducation.com/news/its-a-fact-scientists-more-likely-to-be-socially-inept/152421.article

team building exercises can all holistically help lead to the creation of a superior professional.

## Book IX - The Army on The March (行軍篇第九)

*"He who exercises no forethought but makes light of his opponents is sure to be captured by them."*

[夫惟無慮而易敵者，必擒於人。]

Master Sun here gives another warning against hubris. I might even take it another step further. Even if forethought to system security has been applied, and there are many defenses in place, it is unwise to ever underestimate your opponent. The sophistication of Advanced Persistent Threats (APTs), organized crime groups, and even script kiddies may astound you. Even though the barrier for entry has dropped dramatically, there are still plenty of sophisticated hackers out there, and we must anticipate that any vulnerability that exists, no matter how minor, is a potential avenue for a breach. The idea is not to simply attempt to prevent the breaches – in fact, a breach will likely happen anyway. In 2016,

Ponemon reported[69],[70] that 89% of businesses have experienced a data breach. Again, Defense-in-Depth is the best way to anticipate, contain, and minimize a possible breach.

## Book X – Terrain (地行篇第十)

*"Ground that can be freely traversed by both sides is called accessible. Regarding ground of this nature, be before the enemy in occupying the raised and sunny spots, and carefully guard your line of supplies. Then you will be able to fight with advantage."*

[我以往, 彼以來, 曰通。 通形者, 先居高陽, 利糧道, 以戰則利。]

Most vulnerability scans will report if there are open ports on the firewall. Ideally, they want us to close them all. However, there are many times that we need to have open ports on a firewall to allow various business applications to function properly. Additionally, some servers need to be placed in the DMZ[71] to function. These configurations leave open pathways between the

---

[69] http://www.securitymagazine.com/articles/87117-ponemon-study-89-percent-of-organizations-experienced-data-breaches

[70] https://www2.idexpertscorp.com/sixth-annual-ponemon-benchmark-study-on-privacy-security-of-healthcare-data-incidents

[71] https://en.wikipedia.org/wiki/DMZ_(computing)

local and external network, and thus require additional protections and scrutiny. Especially with a DMZ server, there are many precautions that should be taken. Here are some examples[72]:

1. PRESERVE ISOLATION AS MUCH AS POSSIBLE.

Keep the rules that allow traffic between the DMZ and an internal network as tight as possible. Far too often, administrators simply seeking to troubleshoot a problem will create a rule allowing full access between a DMZ system and a back-end server on the internal network (or the *entire* internal network). This completely defeats the purpose of the DMZ and effectively merges it with the internal network. Instead, one should create specific firewall rules that allow communication only between specific servers on the specific ports required to meet application requirements.

2. PRACTICE GOOD VULNERABILITY MANAGEMENT.

DMZ servers are exposed to the world, so take extra steps to ensure that they are fully patched to deal with the latest security vulnerabilities. Consider daily, automated vulnerability scans of DMZ systems that provide rapid alerts of newly detected vulnerabilities. Additionally, on should consider patching DMZ systems on a much more frequent basis than other protected systems to reduce the

---

[72] http://www.fedtechmagazine.com/article/2012/05/four-tips-securing-network-dmz-fed

window of vulnerability between the time when a patch is released and its application to DMZ servers.

3. USE APPLICATION LAYER DEFENSES FOR ANY EXPOSED SERVICES.

Choose a network firewall that has strong application layer protection, rather than just a port filter. A firewall should have the ability to inspect the content of traffic and block malicious requests. One common example of this is screening inbound web requests for signs of embedded SQL injection attacks, preventing them from even reaching the web server.

4. MONITOR, MONITOR, MONITOR.

The DMZ should be one of the major focuses of an organization's network monitoring efforts. Use intrusion detection systems (IDSs), security incident and event management systems (SIEM), log monitoring and other tools to remain vigilant for signs of an attack (EDR/MDR).

## Book XI - The Nine Situations (九地篇第十一)

*"If asked how to cope with a great host of the enemy in orderly array and on the point of marching to the attack, I should say: "Begin by seizing something which your opponent holds dear; then he will be amenable to your will."*

[敢問: "敵整而將來, 待之若何?"曰:"先奪其所愛, 則聽矣]

It appears that Ransomware was anticipated as far back as the time of Master Sun. One of the reasons we have seen such a huge explosion in the popularity of this attack is because of how wildly effective it is. Generally speaking, it is not much more technically advanced than much other common malware. However, prevent access to someone's critical data, and they will do nearly anything to get it back. In 2017, The Ponemon Institute surveyed[73] 618 IT professionals at small and midsize businesses and found that 51% of companies have already experienced a ransomware attack. Of those victims, an estimated 48% chose to pay an average ransom of $2,500 to get their business files back. In 2015, businesses paid out an estimated $325 million in ransom[74]. In 2016, that number jumped to $1 billion[75], and it continues to grow. By successfully encrypting the data, far too often, the victim panics and winds up paying the ransom. This is a bad idea for several reasons. First, it has been reported that in as many as 25% percent of cases where the ransom was paid, the decryption key was not given. Second, just because you got your files decrypted does not mean that the Ransomware

---

[73] https://www.carbonite.com/globalassets/files-white-papers/ransomware-report.pdf

[74] http://www.lavasoft.com/mylavasoft/company/blog/cryptowall-ransomware-cost-users-325-million-in-2015

[75] http://www.zdnet.com/article/the-cost-of-ransomware-attacks-1-billion-this-year/

authors are removing any of their software from your system. In fact, you have proven to them how valuable your data is, and they may choose to reinfect you again later. Third, these Ransomware campaigns keep happening because people keep paying the ransom. If everyone had better security, browsing habits, and good backups, this problem could go away fairly quickly. By negotiating with terrorists, we only encourage other terrorists to start up campaigns of their own.

# 5. Cassiodorus - Variae Epistolae

Flavius Magnus Aurelius Cassiodorus Senator, also known as simply Cassiodorus, born c. 490, and died around 585, was at different points both statesman and monk, leaving behind a substantial and varied body of literary work. Cassiodorus or, more properly, Senator, born on the paternal estate at Scyllaceum (Squillace) in 490 or somewhat earlier, made his first appearance as councilor to the prætorian prefect about 501. He eventually moved up to the position of chief councilor to Theoderic, King of the Ostrogoths. Among his writings are his letters, which were gathered into twelve books, the "Variæ Epistolæ", at the close of 537. Interestingly, this voluminous correspondence does not contain as much historical information as one would expect. Dates, figures, names of men and places are frequently omitted when opposed to the elegance of style. Several of these letters involve military matters, usually dealing with preparing defenses and keeping armies from pillaging their own people. Many of these letters were written by Cassiodorus on behalf of King Theordoric. The items produced below are only portions of the full letters. This translation is from *The Letters of Cassiodorus, being a condensed translation of the Variae Epistolae of Magnus Aurelius Cassiodorus Senator*, by Thomas Hodgkin (London, 1886).

## Book I, Letter 17: King Theodoric to all the Gothic and Roman inhabitants of Dertona (Tortona)

"*[1] Publicae utilitatis ratione commoniti, quae nos cura semper libenter oneravit, castrum iuxta vos positum praecipimus communiri, quia res proeliorum bene disponitur, quotiens in pace tractatur. munitio quippe tunc efficitur praevalida, si diutina fuerit excogitatione roborata. omnia subita probantur incauta et male constructio loci tunc quaeritur, quando iam pericula formidantur. [2] Adde quod animus ipse in audaciam non potest esse pronus, qui diversa cura fuerit sollicitus. hanc merito expeditionem nominavere maiores, quia mens devota proeliis non debet aliis cogitationibus occupari. quapropter amplectenda res est, quae generalitatis consideratione praecipitur, nec moram fas est incurrere iussionem, quae devotos maxime noscitur adiuvare. [3] Et ideo praesenti auctoritate decernimus, ut domos vobis in praedicto castello alacriter construatis, reddentes animo nostro vicissitudinem rerum, ut, sicut nos vestris utilitatibus profutura censemus, ita tempora nostra ornare vos pulcherrimis fabricis sentianius. tunc enim accidit, ut et sumptus competentes vestris iam penatibus congregare velitis et habitatio vobis non sit ingrata, quam propria potest commendare constructio. [4] Quale est, rogo, in laribus propriis esse, cum durissimas mansiones hostis cogitur sustinere? ille imbribus pateat, vos tecta defendant: illum inedia consumat, vos copia provisa reficiat. sic vobis tutissime constitutis hostis vester ante eventum certaminis fata patiebitur perditoris. constat enim tempore necessitatis illum probari fortissimum virum, qui se per multa non distrahit. nam quis eum habuisse prudentiam putet, si tunc coeperit fabricis operam dare aut penum condere, cum oporteat bella tractare?*

*[…]We have decided that the camp near you shall at once be fortified. It is expedient to execute works of this kind in peace rather than in war. […]*

*The true meaning of* expeditio *shows that the leader of a military expedition should have an unencumbered mind. […]*

*Do you therefore second our efforts by building private houses, in which you will be sheltered, while the enemy (whenever he comes) will be in the worst possible quarters and exposed to all the severity of weather." […]*

By far, a well architected and defensible network is desirable from the start. To come upon a poorly built and designed network already thoroughly in use and attempt to force it into a more secure environment, is far more difficult. Sometimes, we have no choice. However, there are times when it is better to take it all down, focus solely on the task at hand, and rebuild it from scratch. We rarely have this luxury but depending on the sensitivity of the data and systems in use, it may be necessary. Otherwise, you may find yourself breached by a malicious foe while in the middle of upgrades and reconfigurations. Additionally, one can be so beleaguered by constant maintenance issues from old and worn out devices, that we cannot give the attention needed to properly securing the network, and maintaining our due vigilance. Just as an enemy may come at us exhausted from long nights of hacking, we should be well rested and focused on the task at hand.

Book I, Letter 28: King Theodoric to all the Goths and Romans

*"Digna est constructio civitatis, in qua se commendet cura regalis, quia laus est temporum reparatio urbium vetustarum: in quibus et ornatus pacis adquiritur et bellorum necessitas praecavetur. Ideoque*

*praesenti iussione profutura sancimus, ut, si quis cuiuslibet generis saxa in agris suis iacentia muris habuerit profutura, libens animo sine aliqua dilatione concedat, quod tunc magis verius possidebit, cum hoc utilitati suae civitatis indulserit.*

*Most worthy of Royal attention is the rebuilding of ancient cities, an adornment in time of peace, a precaution for time of war.*

*Therefore, if anyone have in his fields stones suitable for the building of the walls, let him cheerfully and promptly produce them. Even though he should be paid at a low rate, he will have his reward as a member of the community, which will benefit thereby."*

Even the ancient Romans were aware of the need for patch management! All kidding aside, even brand new equipment may need to be updated right out of the box. Even as ancient walls fall apart and need stones to fill them, we have to ensure that there is a system in place to monitor, maintain and document the patch status (or lack thereof) of all applicable devices, such as firewalls, routers, workstations, servers, printers, cameras and other Internet of Things (IoT) devices. Having a solid patch management solution and SIEM tool will help greatly with this. Let us examine the WannaCry Ransomware attack in May of 2017. The patch to defend against it had been released in March, two months prior. The critical vulnerability that patch had addressed was EternalBlue, one of the alleged NSA-crafted exploits leaked to the public in April by hacker collective the Shadow Brokers.

It was that exploit that powered WannaCry just a couple months later, and NotPetya a month after that. If the enterprises that were hit had been keeping their systems properly up to date, then the costliest (to this date) ransomware attack in history could have been avoided.

## Book I, Letter 40: King Theodoric to Assuin

*"Ordinatio nostra per moram non debet impediri, ne, quod salubriter constat esse dispositum, per tarditatis vitium incurrat obstaculum. et ideo ante distribuenda sunt arma quam possit flagitare necessitas, ut, cum tempus exegerit, paratiores ad imperata sufficient. ars enim bellandi, si non praeluditur, cum fuerit necessaria, non habetur. proinde illustris sublimitas tua Salonitanis militibus, ut cuique se expediendi facultas obtulerit, pro nostra iussione arma necessaria procurabit, quia fida rei publicae salus est defensor armatus.*

*discat miles in otio, quod perficere possit in bello. animos subito ad arma non erigunt nisi qui se ad ipsa idoneos praemissa exercitatione confidunt. gestiunt vituli certamina, quae impleant aetate robusta: catuli in novellis venationibus ludunt. focos ipsos comprehendere virgultis teneris inchoamus: ceterum si robora primis scintillis adhibeas, igniculum opprimis, quem fovere contendis. sic animi hominum, nisi prius leniter fuerint imbuti, ad hoc, quod tendis, idonei nequeunt reperiri. primordia cuncta pavida sunt et aliter timiditas non tollitur, nisi cum rebus necessariis novitas abrogatur."*

*War needs rehearsal and preparation. Therefore, let your Illustrious Sublimity provide the inhabitants of Salona with arms, and let them practice themselves in the use of them; for the surest safeguard of the Republic is an armed defender.*

*The necessity of drill and practice is shown by the early combats of bullocks, the play-huntings of puppies, the necessity of first kindling a fire with very little sticks, and so forth.*

How can an organization ensure that it will prevent, detect, and respond appropriately to Information Security related threats? Just as the military has wargames, the enterprise IT Security team has a similar model. We call it Red Team and Blue Team exercises, where the Red Team models an attack threat, and the Blue Team models prevention, detection, and response. Network and Web Application Penetration Testers may be employed to deliberately try to hack a network or web application to find all the possible entry points before an enemy does. By utilizing these techniques, the enterprise is better able to understand its risks, and how it might respond in a crisis.

## Book III, Letter 48: King Theodoric to all the Goths and Romans living near the Fort of Verruca

"*Laetitia debet esse cunctorum provida iussio dominantum, quando illud, quod vos debuistis expetere, nos videtis offerre. quid est enim gratius quam humanis rebus cautelam semper adhibere, quae aut fit necessaria aut non gravat esse superfluam? et ideo Leodefrido saioni nostro praesenti delegavimus iussione, ut eius instantia in Verruca castello vobis domicilia construatis, quod a positione sui congruum nomen accepit. [2] Est enim in mediis campis tumulus saxeus in rotunditate consurgens, qui proceris lateribus, silvis erasus, totus mons quasi una turris efficitur, cuius ima graciliora sunt quam cacumina et in mollissimi fungi modo supernus extenditur, cum in inferiore parte tenuetur. agger sine pugna, obsessio secura, ubi nec adversarius quicquam praesumat nec inclusus aliquid expavescat. huic Athesis inter fluvios honorus amoeni gurgitis puritate praeterfluit causam praestans muniminis et decoris: castrum paene in mundo singulare, tenens claustra provinciae, quod ideo magis probatur esse praecipuum, quia feris gentibus constat obiectum. [3] Hoc opinabile munimen, mirabilem securitatem cui desiderium non sit habitare, quam vel externos delectat invisere? et quamquam deo iuvante nostris temporibus provinciam securam credamus, tamen prudentiae nihilominus est cavere etiam quae non putantur emergere. [4] Munitio coaptanda semper in otio est, qua tunc male quaeritur, quando necessaria iudicatur. mergi, quibus nomen ex facto est, cohabitatores piscium, aquatiles volucres futuras tempestates naturaliter praevidentes sicca petunt, stagna derelinquunt. delphini fluctus pelagi metuentes vadosis litoribus immorantur. echini, qui sunt mella carnalia, costatilis teneritudo, croceae deliciae divitis maris, dum futuras tempestates agnoverint, loca mutare cupientes, quia illis pro levitate corporis nandi nulla fiducia est, lapillos, quibus pares possunt esse, complexi, quadam anchorarum ponderatione librati scopulos petunt, quos fluctibus vexandos esse non credunt. [5] Aves ipsae adventu hiemis patrias mutant. ferae pro qualitate temporis cubilia quaerunt. hominum sollicitudo non debet providere quod potest in adversitate requirere? non est in mundo unum: humanae res mutabilitate quatiuntur. et ideo providentia dicitur, ut quae sunt futura tractentur."*

*"It is the duty and the glory of a ruler to provide with wise forethought for the safety of his subjects. We have therefore ordered the Sajo Leodifirid that under his superintendence you should build yourselves houses in the fort Verruca which from its position receives its most suitable name* [in this case, Verruca probably means a steep cliff].

*For it is the midst of the plains a hill of stone roundly arising, which with its tall sides, being bare of woods, is all one great mountain fortress. Its lower parts are slenderer than its summit, and like some softest fungus the top broadens out, while it is thin at bottom. It is a mound not made by soldiers, a stronghold made safe by Nature, where the besieger can try no coup-de-main and the besieged need feel no panic. Past this fort swirls the Adige, that prince of rivers, with the pleasant gurgle of his clear waters, affording a defense and an adornment in one. It is a fort almost unequalled in the whole world, a key that unlocks a kingdom, and all the more important because it bars the invasion of wild and savage nations. This admirable defense what inhabitants would not wish to share, since even foreigners delight to visit it and though by God's blessing we trust that the Province [of Raetia] is in our times secure, yet it is the part of prudence to guard against evils, though we may think they will not arise.*

*Examples of gulls, who fly inland when they foresee a storm; of dolphins, which seek the shallower waters; of the edible sea-urchin, 'that honey of flesh, that dainty of the deep', who anchors himself to a little pebble to prevent being dashed about by the waves; of birds, who change their dwellings when winter draws nigh; of beasts, who adapt their lair to the time of the year. And shall man alone be improvident? Shall he not imitate that higher Providence by which the world is governed?"*

Defense in Depth is a concept still in use that hails from the construction of medieval castles. A King in his keep would have multiple layers of walls, gates, moats and even hills to protect him in case any one layer failed. It understands that no single layer is 100% effective. An attacking force would therefore have to navigate this gauntlet of tasks to successfully lay siege: first, the castle may be on top of a hill, causing the enemy to lose the element of surprise, slow them down, and force them to literally fight an uphill battle. Next, they would need to conquer the town outside the castle, with its own walls, guards and barriers. Then, they would need to break through the main gate, drawbridge and portcullis at the outer wall. Next, they would face boiling oil, water, or hot tar, and arrows. Now, they would need to make their way across the inner bailey, where internal forces could be mustered, and more arrows could rain down from above. Finally, they would need to breach the keep itself. Even the stairs to the top of the keep were a weapon. They were often wound clockwise, so the invading forces would need to use their weapons in their left hands.

So how do we do this in IT? By combining defenses such as SIEM, firewalls, IDS/IPS, SIEM, Endpoint and Gateway Antivirus, heuristics, Data Loss Prevention tools, End User training, Backup and more.

For example, let us assume that a malicious email is sent to an end user with the goal of infecting the network with ransomware. The email could be blocked from entering the enterprise at all by an antispam service or appliance. If it gets past that, it could be stopped and an Intrusion Prevention System.  If it gets past that, the end user could be trained to recognize and delete it. Getting past the end user, it could be stopped by antivirus or heuristic software. After that, it could be prevented by similar software on the server's side.

Then finally, we have multiple backups to draw from, all designed to protect from any single point of failure.

# 6. Niccolò Machiavelli - The Prince

Nicolo Machiavelli was born at Florence on 3rd May 1469. He was the second son of Bernardo di Nicolo Machiavelli, a lawyer of some repute, and of Bartolommea di Stefano Nelli, his wife. Both parents were members of the old Florentine nobility.

His life falls naturally into three periods, each of which singularly enough constitutes a distinct and important era in the history of Florence. His youth was concurrent with the greatness of Florence as an Italian power under the guidance of Lorenzo de' Medici, Il Magnifico. The downfall of the Medici in Florence occurred in 1494, in which year Machiavelli entered the public service. During his official career Florence was free under the government of a Republic, which lasted until 1512, when the Medici returned to power, and Machiavelli lost his office. The Medici again ruled Florence from 1512 until 1527, when they were once more driven out. This was the period of Machiavelli's literary activity and increasing influence; but he died, within a few weeks of the expulsion of the Medici, on 22nd June 1527, in his fifty-eighth year, without having regained office.

Although the light of almost four centuries has been focused on "The Prince," its problems are still debatable and interesting, because they are the eternal problems between the ruled and their rulers. Such as they are, its ethics are those of Machiavelli's contemporaries; yet they cannot be said to be out of date so long as the governments of Europe rely on material rather than on moral forces. Its historical incidents and personages become interesting by reason of the uses which Machiavelli makes of them to illustrate his theories of government and conduct.

Leaving out of consideration those maxims of state which still furnish some European and eastern statesmen with principles of action, "The Prince" is bestrewn with truths that can be proved at every turn. Men are still the dupes of their simplicity and greed, as they were in the days of Alexander VI. The cloak of religion still conceals the vices which Machiavelli laid bare in the character of Ferdinand of Aragon. Men will not look at things as they really are, but as they wish them to be—and are ruined. In politics there are no perfectly safe courses; prudence consists in choosing the least dangerous ones. Then—to pass to a higher plane—Machiavelli reiterates that, although crimes may win an empire, they do not win glory. Necessary wars are just wars, and the arms of a nation are hallowed when it has no other resource but to fight.

It is the cry of a far later day than Machiavelli's that government should be elevated into a living moral force, capable of inspiring the people with a just recognition of the fundamental principles of society; to this "high argument" "The Prince" contributes but little. Machiavelli always refused to write either of men or of governments otherwise than as he found them, and he writes with such skill and insight that his work is of abiding value. But what invests "The Prince" with more than a merely artistic or historical interest is the incontrovertible truth that it deals with the great principles which still guide nations and rulers in their relationship with each other and their neighbors[76].

## Chapter III

*"Perchè sempre, ancorchè uno sia fortissimo in su gli eserciti, ha bisogno del favore de' provinciali ad entrare in una provincial."*

*"For, although one may be very strong in armed forces, yet in entering a province one has always need of the goodwill of the natives."*

Let us assume that a malicious actor has already compromised a network. That may not be enough, even with complete control of the workstations and servers. Hackers know this all too well. A common

---

[76] https://www.gutenberg.org/files/1232/1232-h/1232-h.htm

scam today is to use social engineering to convince the users to wire funds to a wrong account, or buy gift cards, or enter credentials on a website. Sometimes they impersonate a CEO or CFO, but sometime also they go as far as to call the end user and pretend to be their own IT support department! In this case, it is critical to build a good rapport with the user, and to set them at ease. Having their goodwill means they will be far more likely to follow a command that they may be uncomfortable with, or to break their rules and procedures.

*"È ben vero che acquistandosi poi la seconda volta i paesi ribellati, si perdono con più difficultà."*

*"It is very true that, after acquiring rebellious provinces a second time, they are not so lightly lost afterwards."*

Once a business has been compromised, and data or money has been lost, they are sure to be more vigilant in the future. This is why it is critical to evade detection, and to leave virtually no traces when testing against a Blue Team. The last thing an attacker wants is to have fully gained access, then inadvertently revealed himself, and loses it right as he needs it.

In the same way, a hacker that has finally gained deep access has likely learned from experience to make sure he placed several fail safes and alternative means of access. If, as the blue team, you believe you have detected and removed a breach, it is highly advisable to deeply scan and inventory the network traffic and running processes to ensure there are not other means of access remaining. All too often a virus or other malicious application is removed by antivirus, and the system administrator believes their work is done, when there is another application or script running silently in the background, waiting to be triggered.

*"Perchè standovi, si veggono nascere i disordini, e presto vi si può rimediare; non vi stando, s'intendono quando sono grandi, e non vi è più rimedio."*

*"if one is on the spot, disorders are seen as they spring up, and one can quickly remedy them; but if one is not at hand, they are heard of only when they are great, and then one can no longer remedy them."*

There is a constant tradeoff between convenience, security and cost. It is often the case that an enterprise may outsource or centralize its IT support staff. This enables a much lower cost, but the staff may not be as familiar with the specific nuances of each branch office. This can lead to end users more easily being duped by impersonated IT staff, and abnormal activity at the branch level might be missed in the noise of a busy help desk. Malicious activities masquerading as minor issues may also persist for a much longer time before a help desk ticket is created.

System Information and Event Monitoring, or SIEM might be employed to help notice abnormal traffic and other odd network behavior, but Machiavelli's point stands that a local IT staff member might learn more quickly of any issues, and be able to raise alarms before a remote desk can.

*"Perchè i Romani fecero in questi casi quello che tutti i Principi savi debbono fare, li quali non solamente hanno ad aver riguardo alli scandoli presenti, ma alli futuri, ed a quelli con ogni industria riparare; perchè prevedendosi discosto, facilmente vi si può rimediare, ma aspettando, che ti s'appressino, la medicina non è più a tempo, perchè la malattia è diventata incurabile; ed interviene di questa come dicono i medici dell'etica, che nel principio è facile a curare, e difficile a cognoscere, ma nel corso del tempo, non l'avendo nel principio cognosciuta nè medicata, diventa facile a cognoscere e difficile a curare."*

*"Romans did in these instances what all prudent princes ought to do, who have to regard not only present troubles, but also future ones, for which they must prepare with every energy, because, when foreseen, it is easy to remedy them; but if you wait until they approach, the medicine is no longer in time because the malady has become incurable; for it happens in this, as the physicians say it happens in hectic fever, that in the beginning of the malady it is easy to cure but difficult to detect, but in the course of time, not having been either detected or treated in the beginning, it becomes easy to detect but difficult to cure."*

During a breach, time is of the essence, and we must detect it as early as possible. Just as in the previous section, the attacker will only do more damage and drive deeper with time. We have already mentioned SIEM and active log monitoring to death, but this is also where an Intrusion Detection System (IDS), Honeypot and some kind of File Integrity Monitoring (FIM) system to track sensitive file changes would come in. After creating a baseline benchmark of the systems in place, the abnormal traffic becomes much easier to identify.

Here some examples of abnormal activity that blue teams can teach users to watch for:

- Unusually slow Internet or Devices

- Locked out accounts

- Pop-ups and redirected websites when browsing

- Unexpected software installs

- Unexplained changes to files

- Anomalies in normal network traffic patterns

- Abnormal outbound traffic

- Irregular access locations

- Large number of requests for the same objects or files

- Suspicious activity on the network after-hours

- Multiple failed login attempts

- Unknown/unauthorized IP addresses on wireless networks

- Unexplained system reboots or shutdowns

- Services and applications configured to launch automatically

## Chapter V

*"E chi diviene padrone di una città consueta a vivere libera, e non la disfaccia, aspetti di essere disfatto da quella; perchè sempre ha per refugio nella ribellione il nome della libertà, e gli ordini antichi suoi, li quali nè per lunghezza di tempo, nè per beneficii mai si scordano; e per cosa che si faccia o si provvegga, se non si disuniscono o dissipano gli abitatori, non si dimentica quel nome, nè quelli ordini, ma subito in ogni accidente vi si ricorre, come fe' Pisa dopo tanti anni che ella era stata posta in servitù da' Fiorentini."*

*"And he who becomes master of a city accustomed to freedom and does not destroy it, may expect to be destroyed by it, for in rebellion it has always the watchword of liberty and its ancient privileges as a rallying point, which neither time nor benefits will ever cause it to forget. And whatever you may do or provide against, they never forget that name or their privileges unless they are disunited or dispersed, but at every chance they immediately rally to them, as Pisa*

*after the hundred years she had been held in bondage by the*
*Florentines."*

It comes to pass that sometimes, policies that were acceptable in the past are no longer safe. It is not uncommon in smaller businesses to see regular users have local administrator privileges on their computers, or perhaps open network share access to all users. The users easily become accustomed to having such convenient access and control. It will not be easy to convince the users to give up that control, but a word from on high will help. The freedom that eases the burden of management on a system administrator will likely lead to his undoing when disaster strikes. Changing old policies that are no longer secure may be challenging to enforce.

## Chapter VI

*"Debbe un uomo prudente entrare sempre per vie battute da uomini grandi, e quelli che sono stati eccellentissimi, imitare..."*

  *"A prudent man should always follow in the path trodden by great men and imitate those who are most excellent."*

There is wisdom in following the lead from large enterprises, and other successful larger companies by utilizing well known vendors, systems, and services. All too often, a well-intending systems administrator becomes over-enamored with the engineering over the goal. When that happens, we see systems implemented that are so obscure (and often poorly documented) that only the engineer that built it can support it. This is not good from a business standpoint, and certainly not from a security standpoint. A system must be able to be supported even if the implementer is no longer there. Also, who can say what bugs and security holes the system might have? Security through obscurity is not sufficient protection. Even if there are interesting features of other unique or obscure systems, it is often advisable to go with a better-established vendor.

## Chapter XVII

*"Sono tanto semplici gli uomini, e tanto ubbidiscono alle necessità presenti, che colui che inganna, troverà sempre chi si lascerà ingannare."*

*"Men are so simple, and so subject to present necessities, that he who seeks to deceive will always find someone who will allow himself to be deceived."*

Fear, sex, and greed are very powerful motivators. Hackers know this. This is why nearly all email phishing campaigns revolve around one or more of those themes. A recent analysis done by a security vendor showed that an average of 27% of employees would click on test phishing emails at the beginning of their training[77]. Considering that the cost of a bulk spam or phishing campaign is so cheap, even sub-1% response rates make the scams worth it to the attacker. The best possible defense we can have against phishing and other forms of social engineering is to continuously train the end user. They do not need to be certified engineers obviously, however showing a user how to recognize and avoid current and common scams is a simple enough matter. This sort of end user education will have a far greater impact on preventing breaches than any single preventative tool.

## Chapter XXI

*"Nè creda mai alcuno Stato poter pigliare partiti sicuri... La prudenza consiste in saper cognoscere la qualità degli inconvenienti, e prendere il manco tristo per buono."*

*"Never let any Government imagine that it can choose perfectly safe courses... Prudence consists in knowing how to distinguish the character of troubles, and for choice to take the lesser evil."*

Sometimes when architecting a solution, or attempting to resolve a vulnerability, there is no clear answer without drawbacks. It is rare

---

[77] https://blog.knowbe4.com/industries-most-at-risk-of-phishing-attacks-revealed

that we find the 'perfect' solution to any issue, and I.T. is not an exception. Whether it be issues with cost, convenience, security, or the features needed, a project manager needs to be able to determine, occasionally, which solution is the 'least worst.' I have seen situations where this led to decision fatigue, which resulted in some very interesting and odd choices. This is also why it is critical to go over all the pros and cons of a solution before presenting it, so you can anticipate objections, and show that you have thoroughly evaluated a solution. Sometimes, after enough time has passed, and other individuals and teams are working in the environment, they must determine how a less-than-ideal system ever got put into place to begin with. Having the research and reasoning documented is extremely valuable in these situations.

## 7. A Hereditary Book on the Art of War

A Hereditary Book on the Art of War (兵法家伝書) is a Japanese text on the theory and practice of swordsmanship and strategy, written by the samurai Yagyū Munenori in 1632.

Alongside Miyamoto Musashi's The Book of Five Rings, it is one of the preeminent treatises on warfare in classical Japanese literature. Similar to Musashi's contemporary work, Munenori's has garnered appeal for its applicability beyond the warrior paradigm.

*"In general, your posture is intended to prevent your opponent from slashing you. It is like setting up a castle and digging a moat to hold your enemy off. It is not meant to slash your opponent. Don't attack casually, but hold yourself carefully lest you opponent slash you. For these reasons, this is the posture you must learn first.*[78]*"*

I find it fascinating that we speak about one's 'security posture' and here we have an excellent allegory for it. Our stance must first be one of a solid defense, and we should understand the limitations that come with this. In fact, a strong enough posture may in itself cause many battles to be avoided in the first place.

## Chotan Ichimi: Long and Short are One

*"When your opponent is a little too far from you and continues to assess your moves but does not strike, seize an appropriate opportunity to lower your sword, hold it below your belly, and put your left shoulder forward. The moment your opponent strikes at the shoulder, thrust your sword forward with full force and defeat him."*

At times, it is wise to show weakness. To show your opponent a possible opening. Some Kung Fu Sifus I have trained with called this "going fishing." This is a more advanced tactic and can be quite risky. If done well, you can anticipate your opponent's next move and either trick them into being where you want them or take the

---

[78] *The Book of the Shinkage School of Swordsmanship: The Three Elements*

opportunity to learn more about their tactics and techniques. Honeypots, Honeynets, Honeytokens, and even Active Defense techniques align nicely here.

### The Sword of Death

*"Not ignoring a disturbance when governance is good is the basis of the art of war; so is foreseeing a disturbance from the various developments in the state and stopping it before it breaks out."*

How critical it is to have proper tools in place monitoring for anomalies and deviations from the baselines! It is heavily futile to implement an Intrusion Detection System or even any other type of alert monitoring system without properly establishing baselines.

# 8. The Book of Five Rings (五輪書 Go Rin no Sho)

Go Rin no Sho is a text on Kenjutsu (Traditional Japanese Swordsmanship) and martial arts in general and was written by Miyamoto Musashi (宮本 武蔵) about 1645 ad, before he died of lung cancer. There have been various translations of this famous book over the years, and it is studied by far more than just martial artists and people across Asia. Many business leaders find its discussion of conflict and taking the advantage to be relevant to their work in a business context. The modern-day Hyōhō Niten Ichi-ryū school employs it as a manual of technique and philosophy.

Musashi very much believed in being straight forward. For instance, he repeatedly remarks that technical flourishes are excessive, and contrasts worrying about such things with the principle that all technique is simply a method of cutting down one's opponent. He also continually makes the point that the understandings expressed in the book are important for combat on any scale, whether a one-on-one duel or a massive battle. Descriptions of principles are often followed by admonitions to "investigate this thoroughly" through practice rather than trying to learn them by merely reading.

## The Book of Earth

*"The strategist makes small things into big things, like building a great Buddha from a one-foot model... What is big is easy to perceive: what is small is difficult to perceive."*

This is where we see the profits from regular vulnerability scanning and penetration testing. I will give some case studies at the end of this book, but sometimes it is only a very small simple misconfiguration that can lead to a devastating hack. The strategist, or cybersecurity professional, must look for the tiniest of holes and see what damage can come from them. It can be a thankless job, in that the fruits of one's labor may be very difficult to see. But it is the small things that get overlooked regularly, and thus are the most insidious.

## The Book of Water

*"The principles of strategy are written down here in terms of single combat, but you must think broadly so that you attain an understanding for ten-thousand-a-side battles."*

In the SANS teaching material for several of the classes, there is time spent focused on studying the weaknesses of sometimes much older protocols and technologies, even those not still in wide use, such as DES and WEP.

The Data Encryption Standard (DES) is a symmetric-key algorithm for the encryption of electronic data. Although its short key length is of 56 bits, criticized from the beginning, makes it too insecure for most current applications, it was highly influential in the advancement of modern cryptography.

In January 1999, distributed.net and the Electronic Frontier Foundation collaborated to publicly break a DES key in 22 hours and 15 minutes. There are also some analytical results which demonstrate theoretical weaknesses in the cipher, although they are infeasible to mount in practice. The algorithm is believed to be practically secure in the form of Triple DES, although there are theoretical attacks. This cipher has been superseded by the Advanced Encryption Standard (AES). Furthermore, DES has been withdrawn as a standard by the National Institute of Standards and Technology.

Wired Equivalent Privacy (WEP) is a security algorithm for IEEE 802.11 wireless networks. Introduced as part of the original 802.11 standard ratified in 1997, its intention was to provide data confidentiality comparable to that of a traditional wired network. WEP, recognizable by its key of 10 or 26 hexadecimal digits (40 or 104 bits), was at one time widely in use and was often the first security choice presented to users by router configuration tools.

Because RC4 is a stream cipher, the same traffic key must never be used twice. The purpose of an IV, which is transmitted as plain text, is to prevent any repetition, but a 24-bit IV is not long enough to ensure this on a busy network. The way the IV was used also opened WEP to a related key attack. For a 24-bit IV, there is a 50% probability the same IV will repeat after 5,000 packets.

In August 2001, Scott Fluhrer, Itsik Mantin, and Adi Shamir published a cryptanalysis of WEP that exploits the way the RC4 ciphers and IV are used in WEP, resulting in a passive attack that can recover the RC4 key after eavesdropping on the network. Depending on the amount of network traffic, and thus the number of packets available for inspection, a successful key recovery could take as little as one minute. If an insufficient number of packets are being sent, there are ways for an attacker to send packets on the network and thereby stimulate reply packets which can then be inspected to find the key. The attack was soon implemented, and automated tools have since been released. It is possible to perform the attack with a personal computer, off-the-shelf hardware and freely available software such as Aircrack-ng to crack any WEP key in minutes.

Even though these technologies are older examples, we can still learn much from them. Some of the flaws found in WEP are still found in the current specifications for Wi-Fi 6! The idea is that we must be able to take the concepts from the specific examples and apply them to much broader models, much as the overall intent of this book.

*"Strategy is different from other things in that if you mistake the Way even a little you will become bewildered and fall into bad ways."*

It is easy to fall into the trap of planning security by hope and fear, or even falling for the siren song of marketing garbage by so many vendors. This is exactly why so many industries are adopting compliance standards such as DFARS, or the Defense Federal Acquisition Regulation Supplement. The DFARS is a DoD (Department of Defense)-specific supplement to the FAR (Federal Acquisition Regulation). It provides acquisition regulations that are specific to the DoD. DoD government acquisition officials and contractors and subcontractors doing business with the DoD must adhere to the regulations in the DFARS.

The DFARS contains:

- Requirements of law
- DoD-wide policies
- Delegations of FAR authorities
- Deviations from FAR requirements
- Policies and procedures that have a significant effect on the public

The cybersecurity requirements under the DFARS mandate that DoD contractors and subcontractors must implement controls that are specified in the NIST SP (Special Publication) 800-171, "Protecting Controlled Unclassified Information in Nonfederal Information Systems and Organizations." CUI (Controlled Unclassified Information) requires safeguarding in accordance with applicable laws, regulations, and policies.

All contractors and subcontractors processing, storing, or transmitting CUI need to meet minimum security standards specified in the DFARS. Failing to meet these standards can end up in the loss of contracts with the DoD[79].

---

[79] https://www.itgovernanceusa.com/dfars

DFARS is based off of the NIST SP 800-171 security controls, and quite thoroughly describe all aspects of how Information Security systems that handle CUI should be architected, managed, and maintained. By adhering to these well-defined standards, one has a very clear Way to follow. A malicious attack may still be successful, but the defending organization cannot be faulted for properly following the Standard.

## The Book of Fire

*"When the enemy makes a quick attack, you must attack strongly and calmly, aim for his weak point as he draws near, and strongly defeat him. Or, if the enemy attacks calmly, you must observe his movements and, with your body rather floating, join in with his movements as he draws near. Move quickly and cut him strongly. This is Tai No Sen.*

*These things cannot be clearly explained in words. You must research what is written here. In these three ways of forestalling, you must judge the situation. This does not mean that you always attack first; but if the enemy attacks first you can lead him around. In strategy, you have effectively won when you forestall the enemy, so you must train well to attain this."*

Blunt and obvious hacking attempts clearly need to be blocked as quickly as possible. But not all intrusions are alike. Some hackers wish to be subtle, and do not easily let their presence be known.

However, if we have detected them, perhaps with an EDR[80] or IDS[81] solution, we can learn much. By observing the hacker's behavior, perhaps along with other threat-hunting techniques like honeypots, not only might we defend against the current threat, but we can discover new methods, and details about the intruder, such as:

- Their IP address, and possibly their geographic location
- The specific vulnerabilities being targeted
- The types of data they are looking for
- What sensitive information they may already know, such as compromised credentials or hashes
- Their pivoting strategy and techniques

We must be extremely cautious and experienced when allowing an intruder to exist inside even a system that is isolated from our sensitive data, but the rewards can be quite useful. Thus, when the enemy attacks, we may lead him around, and forestall future attacks.

---

[80] Endpoint detection and response (EDR) is a specific type of security focusing on endpoint devices. It is often described as the use of a central data repository to observe and analyze endpoint vulnerabilities and work toward stronger endpoint threat response.

[81] An intrusion detection system (IDS) is a device or software application that monitors a network or systems for malicious activity or policy violations. Any intrusion activity or violation is typically reported either to an administrator or collected centrally using a security information and event management (SIEM) system. They may be host-based (HIDS) or network-based (NIDS).

*"In single combat you must not fix the eyes on the details. As I said before, if you fix your eyes on details and neglect important things, your spirit will become bewildered, and victory will escape you. Research this principle well and train diligently."*

This seems to be a classic issue with engineers in general. I can say this as an engineer myself, and with several family members who are engineers. We tend to want to solve problems. This can lead to getting extremely stuck on a problem because we are too focused on a specific detail, rather than the big picture. I regularly need to train new engineers that our policy is to stop all work after no progress has been made for a certain period of time, and to ask the team to take a look. Often, another set of eyes equally skilled will have some insight that helps move things along. Otherwise, a technician may spend weeks stuck on a problem, barely making progress, feeling extremely discouraged, and ultimately upsetting the end user.

Related to this, I have found engineers to sometimes be so focused on small details that the end work never gets done. Such as spending 5 hours to make a fancy spreadsheet to share very simple data that took 10 minutes to gather and is not ever going to be shown to an end user. I have fallen into this trap myself, and perhaps it is a mildly AD-HD related behavior, but it is key to never lose sight of the overall intent of the work and the end goals.

# 9. Various Sources

## General George S. Patton

*"A pint of sweat will save a gallon of blood."*

Letter (3 March 1944), later published in *War As I Knew It (1947)* Similar expressions were also used in his famous "Speech to the Third Army" in June 1944. The phrase is similar to one attributed to Erwin Rommel, "Sweat saves blood, blood saves lives, and brains saves both", and to an even older one by August Willich: "A drop of sweat on the drill ground will save many drops of blood on the battlefield" from *The Army: Standing Army or National Army?* (1866).

Preparation is not sexy. However, it can be critical to the safety and well-being of an organization. Proper QA, systems review, regular vulnerability assessments, and inspections ensure that when a breach occurs, the attack surface is as small as possible, and our response is swift. This also applies to end user training. No amount of technology will prevent a determined, ignorant user from causing untold damage. While it can be a challenge to convince upper management to devote resources to preventative measures, the rewards are well worth it.

## Giuseppe Tomasi di Lampedusa

Giuseppe Tomasi di Lampedusa was an Italian writer and the last Prince of Lampedusa. He is most famous for his only novel, *Il Gattopardo* (first published posthumously in 1958), which is set in his native Sicily during the Risorgimento. A taciturn and solitary man, he spent a great deal of his time reading and meditating.

*"Se vogliamo che tutto rimanga come è, bisogna che tutto cambi."*

*"If we want things to stay as they are, things will have to change."*

How many objections have been raised by management that center around arguments that 'a lot of money was spent on that project or system, and it's been working fine for years now. Why do we need to change it?'. Threats change. Adversaries change. Like it or not, technology constantly changes, thus the defense of the enterprise, business, or organization must also continue to monitor, plan, and adapt as needed. If we want to keep business running smoothly and maintain the status quo, change is an inevitability.

## Voltaire

Voltaire was a versatile and prolific writer, producing works in almost every literary form, including plays, poems, novels, essays and historical and scientific works. He wrote more than 20,000 letters and more than

2,000 books and pamphlets.[3] He was an outspoken advocate of civil liberties, despite the risk this placed him in under the strict censorship laws of the time. As a satirical polemicist, he frequently made use of his works to criticize intolerance, religious dogma and the French institutions of his day[82].

*"Certainement qui est en droit de vous rendre absurde est en droit de vous rendre injuste."*

*"Certainly, anyone who has the power to make you believe absurdities has the power to make you commit injustices."*

Social Engineering here may be the use of influence and persuasion to deceive people for the purpose of obtaining sensitive information or for the victim to perform an action enabling access to the target, with or without the use of technology, usually by a sense of trust or authority of the attacker. This penetration testing technique preys on human behavior and works to befriend or convince the victim to obtain the information. Social engineering is often an effective way to obtain access and information on without using extensive technical resources to crack password files or actively try to hack a system. Often, people are the weakest links in an organization's security. All the technology in the world cannot protect your network from a user who willingly gives out their password or 'innocently' installs malicious software.

---

[82] https://en.wikipedia.org/wiki/Voltaire

Social engineering is the term used to describe an attempt to manipulate or trick a person into providing valuable information or access to that information. It is the process of attacking a network or system by exploiting the people who interact with that system.

Social engineering often preys on human nature, such as the desire to be helpful, the fear of getting in trouble, or the tendency to trust the people and computers with whom and with which we interact.

Relating to Voltaire's text, an attacker might employ a common social engineering trick: convincing his target that something urgent, and unusual or absurd is going on, and the user needs to act right away. For example, "Hey I'm [CEO's Name]'s new assistant. They told me I need to get access to this file right away." Or, "[CEO's name] is about to get on a plane, but they want you to wire funds to this account ASAP so this deal can go through." It might not take much to trick them into breaking their own policies.

## A Mamluk Manual of War

Umar Ibn Ibrahim al-Awsi Al-Ansari, also known as Ibn al-'Adim, was a scholar and a civil servant in Egypt in the late fourteenth and earlu fifteenth centuries. Before he died in 1408, he composed a manual on the art of warfare, called the Tafrij al-Kurun fi Tadbir al-Hurub. This work is divided up into twenty books, which deal with various topics, such as the qualities of generals and troops, the use of deception to avoid war, precautions to be taken when marching and setting up camp, and how to conduct and defend against sieges.

Book 18, Chapter Two: *About that which is related to the matter of booty.*

*"Among that which should be considered first in this matter is that, if the rout of the enemy actually happens, the men of the army should not divert from the matter of the battle to ·seek plunder and booty. If the rout be a true one, the booty will not escape them; if it be a trick of the enemy, it may lead to some villainy which will overtake the army on the heels of the trick."*

The modern Information Security focused organization is well aware of human nature. They understand that an intruder to a network is likely to seek low hanging fruit by pilfering anything that looks like an easy target first. Patience and observation might lead the attacker to notice that a tempting server is actually a honeypot, or an obviously named file that is easily accessible is a honeytoken.  A honeytoken is a file or object that is planted specifically to be tempting for an intruder to access. This might also be a common port that is not actually in use, or a common account such as 'root' or Administrator'. The object is carefully monitored and is not normally accessed at all. When the file is accessed or copied, alerts are sent out immediately. Even worse, this could lead to the intruder being victim to Active Defense techniques – probably a worst-case scenario for them.

Alexander Pope

*"Hope springs eternal in the human breast: Man never is, but always to be blest."*

There is no end to the abundance of hope in mankind. Hope for money, hope for love, hope for success at heir job. Hackers know this behavior and aim to weaponize it. There is a reason why so-called Nigerian 419, or Advance Fee Scams persist to this day whilst being employed since the 1980s. In fact, the modern scam is similar to the Spanish Prisoner scam which dates back to the late 18th century.[83] In that con, businessmen were contacted by an individual allegedly trying to smuggle someone that is connected to a wealthy family out of a prison in Spain. In exchange for assistance, the scammer promised to share money with the victim in exchange for a small amount of money to bribe prison guards.

One variant of the scam may date back to the 18th or 19th centuries, as a very similar letter, entitled "The Letter from Jerusalem", is seen in the memoirs of Eugène François Vidocq, a former French criminal and private investigator.[84] Another variant of the scam, dating back

---

[83] "An old swindle revived; The "Spanish Prisoner" and Buried Treasure Bait Again Being Offered to Unwary Americans". The New York Times. 20 March 1898. p. 12.

[84] *Vidocq, Eugène François (1834). Memoirs of Vidocq: Principal Agent of the French Police until 1827. Baltimore, Maryland: E. L. Carey & A. Hart. p. 58.*

to circa 1830, appears very similar to what is passed via email today: "Sir, you will doubtlessly be astonished to be receiving a letter from a person unknown to you, who is about to ask a favour from you...", and goes on to talk of a casket containing 16,000 francs in gold and the diamonds of a late marchioness.[85]

Human behavior has not significantly changed in all that time. Nor even has knowledge of the scam prevented scores of people from being duped into falling for it every year.

*"A little learning is a dangerous thing; Drink deep, or taste not the Pierian spring."* Also: *"Fools rush in where angels fear to tread."*

If one is to begin study of a subject for the sake of professional advancement or practical implementation, one must be thorough in their studies, or they may as well not begin at all. Much damage has been done, and continues to occur, from persons proclaiming their expertise and do not yet understand the depth of their ignorance. Often, the environments these persons are in charge of contain many vulnerabilities complex and varied, as well as many issues with configurations and policies.

---

[85] Harris, Misty (June 21, 2012). "Nigerian email scams royally obvious for good reason, study says". The Province.

*"Speak what you think to-day in words as hard as cannon balls, and to-morrow speak what tomorrow thinks in hard words again, though it contradict every thing you said to-day."*

Technology is constantly changing! Because of this, the standards must change as well. Cybersecurity is never a 'set it and forget it' type of system. We must build a culture of constant revision and confirmation. The NIST Cybersecurity lifecycle describes a wheel with the following sections:

1. Identify
2. Protect
3. Detect
4. Respond
5. Recover

Then back to the first item. Because the technology changes, the threats change. Even if the technology did not change, it can take decades for even severe vulnerabilities to be discovered sometimes. OpenBSD's head bug took 37 years and 2 months to fix[86]!

---

[86] http://cvsweb.openbsd.org/cgi-bin/cvsweb/src/usr.bin/head/head.c?rev=1.18&content-type=text/x-cvsweb-markup

In August 1977, future Sun Microsystems co-founder Bill Joy wrote the head function, used to display the first lines of a file, for 1BSD, the initial release of the Berkeley Software Distribution (BSD), a Unix derivative. Joy's original code was later inherited by forks and sub-forks of BSD, such as 386BSD, NetBSD, and OpenBSD.

15 years after Joy wrote head, in 1992, it was discovered that, under certain circumstances, it could raise an error, due to the use of a function called freopen to open files and streams for reading, which didn't play nicely with stdin. Keith Bostic applied to the fix to 4.4BSD, but the bug remained in some BSD-derivatives, such as NetBSD, which was based on 386BSD in 1993, itself forked from 4.3BSD in 1989, which didn't have Bostic's fix. Subsequently, the bug was present when OpenBSD was created from NetBSD in 1996. In October 2014, Ingo Schwarze finally rectified the 18-year-old problem by merging Bostic's 22-year-old fix into OpenBSD.

How about a 33-year-old buffer overflow vulnerability?

In 1975, Stephen Johnson working at AT&T Bell Labs, developed Yet Another Compiler-Compiler (YACC), a tool for generating the parser portion of a language compiler. Johnson's YACC, first written in the B programming language then in C, was the default parser-generator on Unix systems for years. It was first included with the Sixth Edition of Unix, released by Bell Labs in May, 1975 and Johnson's YACC code was passed down to many later Unix derivatives, such as the BSD branch of the Unix tree.

In 2008, Otto Moerbeek, an OpenBSD developer, was trying to track down the reason that compiling some large C++ programs on Sparc64 systems would fail with an Internal Compiler Error. It turned out that a new memory allocation routine that he had written wasn't the cause; instead, Johnson's YACC code was to blame. Moerbeek's new malloc code was able to detect that Johnson's YACC would cause a buffer overflow under certain conditions on Sparc64 systems only. He fixed the problem in OpenBSD a little over 33 years after Johnson's YACC code was first released[87].

We must continually be working on phase one: Identify, even long after the code is laid to bed, and the systems have been implemented.

## Helmuth Karl Bernhard von Moltke (The Elder)

"Kein Operationsplan reicht mit einiger Sicherheit über das erste Zusammentreffen mit der feindlichen Hauptmacht hinaus.[88]"

*"No plan of operations extends with certainty beyond the first encounter with the enemy's main strength."*

Often mangled into "No plan survives the first battle," this is a great advocation to first, recognize that plans fail, but also to have contingencies. We have talked at length thus far about Defense in

---

[87] http://undeadly.org/cgi?action=article&sid=20080708155228

[88] Militärische Werke, Band 2, Teil 2. Mittler & Sohn Berlin 1900

Depth, and this statement also explains why we need thorough Incident Response Plans (IRPs) that attempt to account for many various possible outcomes. Even if we have a solid plan to respond to a specific type of event, does it cover all the ways it can fail? For example, during a ransomware attack, critical information is distributed to the team and contractors via email. However, the email may have been compromised by the attacker already, so out-of-band communications are necessary.

## Louis Pasteur

"Dans les champs de l'observation, le hasard ne favorise que les esprits prepares.[89]"

*"In the fields of observation, chance favors only the prepared mind."*

Tabletop exercises between red and blue teams are critical to ensuring the smooth operation of information security teams at any organization. By doing these exercises, one discovers all the small issues that may prevent them from working properly in the case of a real-life event. Additionally, by preparing as much as possible for as many

---

[89] L. Pasteur, "Discours prononcé à Douai, le 7 décembre 1854, à l'occasion de l'installation solennelle de la Faculté des lettres de Douai et de la Faculté des sciences de Lille" (Speech delivered at Douai on December 7, 1854 on the occasion of his formal inauguration to the Faculty of Letters of Douai and the Faculty of Sciences of Lille), reprinted in: Pasteur Vallery-Radot, ed., Oeuvres de Pasteur (Paris, France: Masson and Co., 1939), vol. 7, p. 131

outcomes as possible, very little is left up to chance. Many cases of "oh, we got lucky" is due to actually having been well prepared.

## Frederick the Great[90]

"Wer alles defendieren will, defendieret gar nichts!"

*"He who defends everything defends nothing."*

This statement is particularly true as an organization scales upwards in size and complexity. Part of the operation maturity of an information security team is knowing when to begin segregating duties to new job roles. As things grow, it will simply become too much for any individual to be able to adequately monitor, or even to have the proper training to do so.

## Ron Swanson

*"Never half-ass two things. Whole-ass one thing."*

In accordance with the wisdom of The Philosopher, we are urged to fully complete one task before attempting another. Partially implementing a new information security system can at times be worse than not implementing one at all. Poor configurations and new vulnerabilities may arise in the meantime and must be corrected swiftly.

---

[90] AKA Friedrich II. von Preußen

# Practical Applications

Now that we have had a chance to explore wisdom from some of the greatest tactical and strategic thinkers in history, how can we put this into practice? Abstract historical lessons and philosophy holds its own merits, but we have actual networks to defend here. Below, I will include some examples from my own experience, but also from notable large-scale incidents as well.

## Case Study 1: Entertainment Company X

With the examples from my personal experience, I will be redacting the names of the companies and individuals involved.

In this first case, I had been contracted to perform a Penetration Test and CIS Top 20 Security Controls Assessment. This client works in the entertainment industry, and regularly interacts with all the major studios, as well as prominent celebrities and political figures. They had been fairly confident of their security "because everyone used Macs." During scoping we agreed to perform a Gray Box Test. In this scenario, the penetration tester is given limited information about the environment. It was disclosed that all users had company issued Macs, and the network was segmented into VLANs, so that the VoIP data, the wired data, and the wireless data were completely inaccessible from each other. There was no server on the network, except for a Mac Mini that was being used for file sharing. The Mac Mini was locked down with strict file access permissions.

Upon beginning the engagement, I made my way to the front of the building. There was a security desk which required all guests to sign in. I timed my entry to coincide with the beginning of the work day, so it was as busy as possible. I waited to approach until a group of employees of the building were entering, and I joined the group, walking right past security into the elevators. These elevators required a badge to be scanned to be able to select a floor, so that contractors and guests would be required to have an escort. Once inside the elevator, I pantomimed looking for my card, then asked a younger employee if she could swipe me in since, I had left my card in my car by mistake. It worked, and I was on my way to the target's floor. Once on the floor, I started checking Wi-Fi strength from the elevator to their door. I found that the signal from their Wi-Fi fully extended most of the hallway, and had excellent coverage, even into a bathroom that was not kept locked.

I continued to a spare desk and began my work in earnest. Since a narrative was already beginning to write itself in my head, I decided to focus on the Wi-Fi first. I started up my wireless sniffing setup with tcpdump, kismet, and a Wi-Fi Pineapple to see if I could capture any WPA 4-way handshakes. After waiting a while, I had no luck. All of the wireless clients had already associated for the morning. I decided to make my own luck and initiated a deauthentication attack using the MDK3 tool against a couple of devices. Surely enough, I was able to capture the 4-way handshake when they tried to rejoin the wireless network. Once it had that, I converted it for use with hashcat, a popular and efficient cracking tool on my personal cracking/cryptomining rig at my office. After some trial and error, I eventually was able to crack the WPA PreShared Key (PSK) and could join the employee wireless SSID.

At this point, I began to scan the network for hosts and ports of interest. I discovered what appeared to be devices running Java as their OS on the network. Suspecting these were phones, I captured network traffic with Wireshark for a period, and realized I had captured VoIP traffic. In the interest of privacy, I did not extract the phone conversations out of my capture file, although it would be trivial to do so. Apparently, the wireless, wired, and phone networks were not separated at all!

During my scanning of the hosts on the network, I did find the Mac Mini server, and in fact it was properly locked down with file and share permissions. Except for a folder called "downloads." It appears this folder was created for temporary storage of trivial materials. However, I found a backup of the VP's entire email client database. I later found out that their IT guy had been setting up a new laptop for the VP and had exported a copy of her email to this folder so he could easily copy it to the new laptop. Inside the archive I found voicemails sent as email attachments, emails to and from celebrities and political figures, and even a copy of the online mailing list database.

Essentially, only one actual 'hack' happened: the crack of the wireless key. With just that and some misconfigurations, I was able to demonstrate that an unknown person could walk in from the street, set up in a restroom stall, hack into the network, and have full access to all network traffic, live phone calls, and their entire client database. Not so good.

So, what principles from our study so far could we apply here? There were clearly failures of Defense-in-depth, Social Engineering, proper isolation, baselining, and detection.


## Case Study 2: Union X


In this case study, I was contracted by a union based in Hollywood. They had a solid relationship with an existing Managed IT Services Provider (MSP), and were very security focused. For this case, it was decided to perform a crystal-box penetration test, where I would have detailed knowledge of the environment. My activities would be similar to those of an in-house Red Team member, and we started from an assumption of existing compromise. Just to prove the point, I asked if I could have access to a sample workstation so I could try to compromise it by email. Later in the test, I used Metasploit to create a reverse TCP shell, and used MSFVenom and the Veil Framework to hide my malware from matching existing antivirus signatures. It worked, and I was able to successfully gain a remote shell to the workstation.

During day 1 of the project, I drove up to the squawk box that was in front of the gate blocking entry to their locked, private parking lot. I told the person on the other end I was there to meet Person X. Their name, bio, and contact info were all on the website for the public to see. I asked if I could use the parking lot so that I could avoid needing to find street parking. The person let me in without any verification of my identity. This business used RFID cards to control access to all external doors of the building, so I wasn't sure exactly what method I would use to gain access. It turned out that my job would be fairly easy that day, as I saw one of the doors had been propped open. I grabbed my backpack and walked in. a little further down the hallway, I saw several contractors mounting a TV in the conference room. Apparently, they had been working all morning, and simply propped the door open for convenient access to the tools in their truck. I walked an entire circuit of the bottom floor to see if my presence would be challenged by anyone. I was not.

Ultimately, internal network security was quite decent compared to the state I often find businesses in. I was able to perform pass-the-hash attacks due to a lack of defense to Mimikatz, however. I also found that I could reliably crash and reboot two key switches by sending specially crafted 10kb packets to them. Finally, I also found that Active Directory was not being well maintained, as there were users and computers present that had not been active for years.

So let's put this together into a narrative. An unknown attacker could either gain remote access by tricking a user into opening a malicious attachment to an email, or possibly walk in off the street. From there, either with local access to a workstation or remote, he could gain domain administrative credentials with pass-the-hash, and give an old, unused computer and user administrative access. In this way, he could remain active in the network without necessarily raising any alarms, and could cause both network disruption and data exfiltration.

What wisdom from history can we apply here?

## Case Study 3: Equifax

In 2017, Equifax, an American company that deals with credit scores, was hacked. The sensitive personal information of nearly 145 million[91] people from the United States, Canada, and the European Union were compromised. The breach occurred on an internet facing web server that ran their credit entry dispute application. The server was discovered by the attackers possibly by accident as part of a general scan across the internet of a newly discovered vulnerability in Apache Struts, a framework to develop web applications using Java. This vulnerability allowed for remote code execution (as bad as it gets!) due to failing to properly perform input validation on data that end users could pass along to it. A patch came out for the vulnerability after it was

---

[91] www.businessinsider.com/how-equifax-compares-to-biggest-hacks-of-all-time-chart-2017-9?r=UK&IR=T

publicly disclosed, Equifax did not install it. Only two days after the critical patch was released, their server was compromised on March 9th. It was later determined that data was already being exfiltrated by March 13th and continued to July 30th. Equifax did not even realize they had been breached until July 29th, then waited until September 7th to publicly report the breach[92].

This attack affected all three parts of the CIA Triad, the critical tenets of Information Security: that we must protect the Confidentiality, Integrity and Availability of sensitive information.

By breaching the servers the hackers could modify the data on them, violating its integrity, by viewing and stealing the data, they violated its confidentiality, and by the subsequent need for Equifax to shut down access to those servers, the availability of access to the data was disrupted.

Since the attackers had full reign to do whatever they pleased on the server without being detected from March until July, this also points us to that key concept in Information Security: "**prevention is ideal, but detection is a must**." It is possibly forgivable that the servers could not have been patched in time, but without any sort of proper detection mechanisms in place, the attackers had four days moving about the system and running various commands and scans before they even

---

[92] https://arstechnica.com/information-technology/2017/09/massive-equifax-hack-reportedly-started-4-monthsbefore-
it-was-detected/

started to exfiltrate data, then still had months after that before they were discovered. Because the vulnerability they exploited allowed for system level access, they were able to create over 30 different remote shells to ensure they had many different means of persistently maintaining their access.

What made things worse was that the servers that were compromised also contained files with credentials and other information for internal Equifax servers. The information that was pilfered included credit card information, social security numbers, names, addresses, birth dates, and even driver's license numbers.

The aftermath was almost comically terrible. It came out that the Chief Security Officer for Equifax had no formal Information Security education, but rather a music degree, and she was promptly thrown to the wolves and fired. Equifax offered free credit monitoring services to all affected, at a cost of around $20-$30 per person to the company. They opened an entirely new call center to handle to the madness, and at significant cost. But, perhaps most ridiculous of all, they sent out a bulk email, and put a link up on their website directing people to go to www.equifaxsecurity2017.com for more information. Not a subdomain of their main site, but a URL that absolutely looks like a phishing link from a spam email. On that site, users needed to enter their last name and last 6 digits of their Social Security Number, which made it seem even more suspicious, in order to confirm if their data had been leaked. *Even worse*, the site seemed to be completely worthless, as a security researcher entered junk data, such as "test" as a last name and

"123456" and was informed by the site that he had been impacted by the breach.

Congress has called the entire incident "entirely preventable" and one congressman called Equifax executives "stupid." Outside of Capitol Hill, the conversation was a lot less polite. Two years on, no one knows who stole that mountain of sensitive data or what they've done with it.

Wall Street is taking notice of the consequences. In 2019, Moody's, the financial rating service, downgraded Equifax from a "stable" to a "negative" outlook due to the high level of cybersecurity spending and litigation that comes as a direct result of the 2017 breach. It is the first time cybersecurity was cited as the reason for an outlook change, CNBC reported[93].

The numbers add up to a fortune, even for a massive corporation like Equifax. Lawsuits and investigations have cost $690 million in the first quarter of 2019 alone, which Moody's cited as one of the reasons for its outlook downgrade. Moody's expects $400 million more spent in each of the next two years and then a $250 million bill in 2021.

To drive home the point about Equifax's spectacular blunder, here are the highlights from a 2018 congressional report[94] on the incident:

---

[93] https://www.cnbc.com/2019/05/22/moodys-downgrades-equifax-outlook-to-negative-cites-cybersecurity.html

[94] https://oversight.house.gov/wp-content/uploads/2018/12/Equifax-Report.pdf

**Entirely preventable.** Equifax failed to fully appreciate and mitigate its cybersecurity risks. Had the company taken action to address its observable security issues, the data breach could have been prevented.

**Lack of accountability and management structure.** Equifax failed to implement clear lines of authority within their internal IT management structure, leading to an execution gap between IT policy development and operation. Ultimately, the gap restricted the company's ability to implement security initiatives in a comprehensive and timely manner.

**Complex and outdated IT systems.** Equifax's aggressive growth strategy and accumulation of data resulted in a complex IT environment. Both the complexity and antiquated nature of Equifax's custom-built legacy systems made IT security especially challenging.

**Failure to implement responsible security measurements.** Equifax allowed over 300 security certificates to expire, including 79 certificates for monitoring business critical domains. Failure to renew an expired digital certificate for 19 months left Equifax without visibility on the exfiltration of data during the time of the cyberattack.

**Unprepared to support affected consumers.** After Equifax informed the public of the data breach, they were unprepared to identify, alert and support affected consumers. The breach website and call centers were immediately overwhelmed, resulting in affected consumers being unable to access information necessary to protect their identity.

There is an awful lot to unpack here, but what wisdom from the sources we've seen could we apply that would have prevented or mitigated some of this?

## Case Study 4: Wannacry

The Wannacry ransomware attack of 2017 is considered, at the time of this writing, to be the costliest and most widespread virus of all time (so far). It infected around an estimated 230,000 systems across 150 countries. This attack began around May 12th in Asia and used a vulnerability in Microsoft's SMB protocol for systems that were exposed to the internet[95]. As in the prior example, a patch had already been released to fix the vulnerability, although this time, it had been available for two months before the attack spread. Researchers discovered that this ransomware was created by a North Korean group and utilized tools that the NSA had created. A hacking group called The Shadow Brokers had previously gained access to compromised NSA assets, including an entire catalog of hacking tools, some of which were deployed here. Wannacry, once it had infected a system, would ping out to the internal network, and look for other systems to infect, then use the kill command to disable other security tools, such as antivirus, finally using

---

[95] http://www.news.com.au/technology/online/hacking/massive-cyber-attack-creates-chaos-around-the-world/newsstory/
b248da44b753489a3f207dfee2ce78a9

the exec command to push arbitrary code to other systems, continuing the cycle of infection.

I happened to be at the SANS Security West Conference right as this event was breaking. It was an amazing experience, as we had an emergency session, and hundreds of Information Security experts all piled into a room and started sharing their experience and knowledge. Several experts led the discussion and covered what was known up to that point in great detail. Subsequently, because of my experience here, I wound up coming into contact with a request from the FBI to our community asking for any help with information. I got in contact with him, and then the FBI's Special Agent in charge of the WannaCry investigation. I was able to share what small knowledge I had picked up from the event and got permission in advance to put him in touch with the experts who had been leading the discussion. So at least in some small way, I was able to assist in the investigation.

What was shocking here was three things: one, that system administrators allowed a critical vulnerability to go unchecked for two months, two, that SMB was allowed to be enabled on internet-accessible servers, and three, that there were not tools employed to detect these commands being run that should certainly raise red flags. But businesses across the globe of all sizes failed to do any of these steps, became infected, and spread the plague.

Hindsight is 20/20 as they say, so what principles could have been followed to employ preventative measures?

# Appendix I

The following is a paper I wrote in partial satisfaction of the requirements by the SANS Institute for their SEC560 GPEN Gold certification.

# Piso Mojado

**A Ubiquitous Hole in Physical Security**

**An InfoSec Research Paper by Kenneth May**

## Introduction

As I continue this journey down the path of increasing my knowledge and skills in the field of Information Security, I found myself looking through my past experiences for topics to research further. I wished to produce this paper in order to both further the general knowledge of our Information Security community, and also to satisfy the requirements for increasing my SANS GSEC certification to Gold Level. But where does one start, when looking for a subject, when so many topics have been spoken about already? While I was reading through the available security whitepapers out there[96], I found many, many papers talking about the usefulness of certain tools, or how to exploit certain software vulnerabilities. I found papers on Information Security theory, but found many of them difficult to apply to the real word experience. That brought me back to my own past experiences, and all the little things I have noticed along the way, in my various jobs and contracts throughout the years. What have I seen that stood out to me, and would be applicable and pertinent to many businesses and organizations? Which of those experiences might not be well known or understood? An observation I made during my early years as an independent contractor came back to me. After some research, it seems there is still not much

---

[96] The SANS Reading Room is an excellent resource:

https://www.sans.org/reading-room/

discussion on this subject, so I will discuss it here, that knowledge of this vulnerability might be finally addressed more commonly in the business and Information Security community.

Thesis

I recall an incident when I was working as a contractor for Hewlett Packard, some years back. I was a team lead for a group of technicians who were doing end-of-warranty workstation replacements for several high profile financial firms. As I was walking the building to deploy the workstations, I was required to be escorted by a security guard through all the various sections of the building. I was given a keycard that would let me into only some areas, but not others. These physical security barriers were quite disruptive to being able to do my work, and added a lot of time to the overall project. It was as I was being escorted into another section yet again, I noticed that a member of the cleaning crew, with their ever-present cleaning cart, was entering and exiting the same sections I was, using her own keycard, and without any escort. Out of curiosity (and some frustration) I asked the guard who that was. He said he had no idea. Just another member of the cleaning crew. How convenient for them! But how was this ok? I was a certified, contracted, background-checked and identity-verified team leader for an expected project. I had less access than this person from some other company, on no schedule, completely unknown to the security team. Was this person background checked? Were they actually from the cleaning company? Did this person have a valid immigration status or even speak English? They were not even required to sign in and out of the vendor log, as I was. This was no fly-by-night organization; this was a Fortune 500 company. After continuing to work similar projects for different companies, in different cities and states across the country, it came to me that this was a major security hole, and it was being completely ignored. Therefore, what I seek to show in this document, is this: *that there is an entire workforce of individuals, specifically from at-risk demographics, who are being given unfettered physical access to critical business infrastructure, with virtually no oversight or regulation.*

An Overview of Security Concepts

Before we dive too deeply into why this is truly an issue, there are several concepts from Information Security Theory that we should be looking to for guidance when determining an acceptable guideline for the security of a given business' infrastructure. There are many theories and principles out there, but we will only be looking at a small subset that applies to the topic at hand.

The first is the Principle of Least Privilege, a concept first put forth in 1974 by Jerome Saltzer[97]. Wikipedia says: The principle means giving a user account only those privileges which are essential to that user's work. For example, a backup user does not need to install software: hence, the backup user has rights only to run backup and backup-related applications. Any other privileges, such as installing new software, are blocked. The principle applies also to a personal computer user who usually does work in a normal user account, and opens a privileged, password protected account (that is, a superuser) only when the situation absolutely demands it.

When applied to users, the terms least user access or least-privileged user account (LUA) are also used, referring to the concept that all user accounts at all times should run with as few privileges as possible, and also launch applications with as few privileges as possible. Software bugs may be exposed when applications do not work correctly without elevated privileges.

The principle of least privilege is widely recognized as an important design consideration in enhancing the protection of data and functionality from faults (fault tolerance) and malicious behavior

[97] Saltzer, Jerome H. (1974). "Protection and the control of information sharing in multics". *Communications of the ACM* **17** (7): 389. doi:10.1145/361011.361067. ISSN 0001-0782.

(computer security).[98] Of course, these principles readily apply to people, as well as user accounts. Mary the secretary does not need access to the company safe. Bob the doorman does not need to have access to the executive lounge, no matter how much he might desire it. A member of the cleaning crew does not need access to the server room, if all they do is clean the offices.

Another principle of security design we should examine, is that of Defense in Depth.  According to Viega and McGraw[99]:

The idea behind defense in depth is to manage risk with diverse defensive strategies, so that if one layer of defense turns out to be inadequate, another layer of defense will hopefully prevent a full breach. This principle is well known, even beyond the security community; for example, it is a famous principle for programming language design to have a series of defenses so that if an error isn't caught by one, it will probably be caught by another.

…

The defense in depth principle may seem somewhat contradictory to the "secure the weakest link" principle, since we are essentially

[98] https://en.wikipedia.org/wiki/Principle_of_least_privilege (accessed 07/27/2016)

[99] [Viega 02] in Chapter 5, "Guiding Principles for Software Security," in "Principle 2: Practice Defense in Depth" from pages 96-97:1

saying that defenses taken as a whole can be stronger than the weakest link. However, there is no contradiction; the principle "secure the weakest link" applies when components have security functionality that does not overlap. But when it comes to redundant security measures, it is indeed possible that the sum protection offered is far greater than the protection offered by any single component.

And finally, According to NIST [NIST 01] in Section 3.3, "IT Security Principles," from page 9:

Implement layered security (ensure no single point of vulnerability). Security designs should consider a layered approach to address or protect against a specific threat or to reduce a vulnerability. For example, the use of a packet-filtering router in conjunction with an application gateway and an intrusion detection system combine to increase the work-factor an attacker must expend to successfully attack the system. Adding good password controls and adequate user training improves the system's security posture even more.

The need for layered protections is especially important when commercial-off-the-shelf (COTS) products are used. Practical experience has shown that the current state-of-the-art for security quality in COTS products does not provide a high degree of protection against sophisticated attacks. It is possible to help mitigate this situation by placing several controls in series, requiring additional work by attackers to accomplish their goals.

As before, all these information security concepts are as readily applied to people and physical systems, as they are to software and users.

See the following diagram, for a visual representation of this concept:

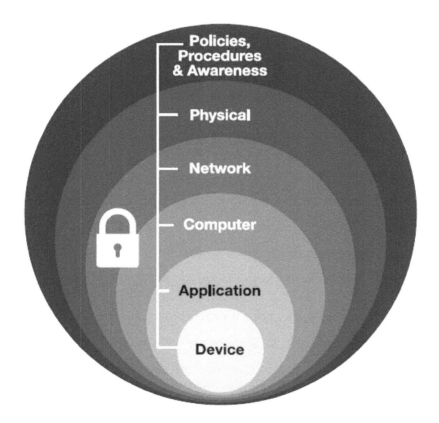

Clearly, the primary focus for the discussion here, is the physical layer of security. All the IT spending in the does not help much, if one can simply walk into an office and physically access a workstation or server. Disabling USB ports, and full-drive encryption help, but come with additional performance and convenience burdens. However, even those protections can be bypassed by something like a simple hardware keylogger installed surreptitiously.

Who are these people?

According to the United States Bureau of Labor Statistics,[100] there are roughly 2,360,000 persons working in the janitorial or building cleaning professions, growing at a pace of about 6%. 2.3 million people is nothing to laugh at, and from all accounts, it seems to be an industry that is growing well. However, 55% of managers are concerned about their staff's quality of work, 45% are concerned about their motivation or lack of interest, and 34% are concerned with employee turnover[101]. So, this industry is telling us that we have a fleet of people who aren't doing great work, aren't motivated, and quit easily.

---

[100] http://www.bls.gov/ooh/building-and-grounds-cleaning/janitors-and-building-cleaners.htm

[101] http://www.statista.com/statistics/324481/challenges-in-managing-a-cleaning-staff-us/

Demographically, between 17% to 23% of the total undocumented immigrant population living in the United States work in the cleaning industry [102]. In addition to this population offering an abundant source of inexpensive labor,[103] janitorial work is mostly undertaken at night, making it an appealing option for janitorial companies to employ undocumented workers[104],[105] seeking clandestine employment. Cheating the system is not new, but many in the cleaning industry feel the problem is getting worse. There are plenty of reasons for the worsening situation, but probably the biggest is economic woes. A poor economy in recent years has created an environment that rewards contractors for lowering prices, even to below what is legally possible. Another trend in the industry that contributes to the problem is consolidation and franchising. National cleaning companies bid on a large number of chains with multi-state offices and then use small, local service firms as subcontractors to complete the work. The problem is that many of these big players want the work done for impossibly low rates.

---

[102] Weltin, Dan (2010-05-21).
http://www.cleanlink.com/cp/article/Immigration-Reform-Theres-Always-An-Excuse--12050

[103] Mollenkamp, Becky (2011-04-11). "Illegal Subcontracting Bad Apples: Illegal subcontracting's continuing impact on the BSC industry"

[104] Ridgely, Lisa (2010-03-01). "Overdue Diligence: How BSCs can avoid hiring undocumented workers"

[105] Miriam, Jordan (2011-08-15). "Immigration Audits Drive Illegal Workers Underground: ABM Caught for Employing illegal immigrants". online.wsj.com

Many such immigrants have even started their own janitorial companies using fictitious business licenses[106] and false identification[107],[108] information. Further, one report showed that at least 3% of job applicants had misdemeanors, and 7% had felonies[109].

This is seriously worrisome to think about. Now, I'm sure the vast majority of these people are good, hard-working folks, who are simply trying to provide for themselves and their families. Yet the point here is that this group is an at-risk group, and are being given carte-blanche access to every part of our nation's infrastructure.

One of the pieces of information is sought the most eluded me. I could not find research that showed what percentage of contracted cleaning companies actually perform background checks. It might not be useful data, even if such a study has been done. If it is self-reported data, the companies could simply be lying about performing the checks, and less reputable companies would not be likely to respond to such a survey at all.

---

[106] Mortensen, Ronald (June 2009). "Backgrounder: Illegal, but Not Undocumented Identity Theft, Document Fraud, and Illegal Employment"
[107] Mims, Brian (12/05/2006). "5 Illegal Immigrants Charged in Fake ID Scheme"
[108] Yost, Denise (2011-07-15). "Illegal Immigrant Arrested For Allegedly Making Fake IDs"
[109] http://www.cleanlink.com/bscai/article/Contract-Cleaners-Should-Conduct-Employee-Background-Checks--19342

A quick story

In fact, while researching this paper, I had a friend, who happens to be an Information Security Instructor, share the following story with me. As a youth, he was looking for easy work, and saw an ad in the paper for work with a cleaning company. It seemed like a good opportunity for him, as it was easy work being done after hours. No background check, no drug check, no skills required. He was just out of high school, so, why not? He got the job, and did not really care about the work, in part due to the recklessness of his youth. Well, he wound up getting fired from his company eventually. Not because he would regularly look through desk drawers out of curiosity. Not for sneaking food from the fridge. No, it was because he was using office copiers to print up flyers for his own interests. The only reason he got caught was that one of the maids reported him. The businesses he was servicing likely would never have known, had it not been for a coworker reporting him.

Back to reality

This is only an anecdotal episode, of just one person's experience. However, let's look at the bigger picture. This is likely a very common story, for many workers also in this position. Entry level, minimum wage positions are far more likely to encourage an employee to make poor decisions just like this. With this in consideration, and considering the demographic makeup of the people staffing these firms, and the predominance of foreign-born workers, it is not a great leap of logic to see that there is risk here. If an advanced persistent threat, such as an unfriendly foreign government, reached out to a worker and offered them a few hundred dollars to attach a malicious USB drive to a server, or VIP's workstation, it would not be shocking to us for them to accept that offer.

But do we have any evidence that these possible attack vectors are being actively utilized? The answer is unabashedly yes. In 2006, a man working as a janitor successfully stole, and tried to sell nuclear industry secrets[110]. He thought he was selling the information to the French, and confessed to the authorities when caught: "*I couldn't sell it to the North Koreans, because it might wind up being used against us,*" Oakley told the man whom he believed to be an emissary from the French government. "*I couldn't sell it to the Arabs for the same reason. But you guys already got nuclear power. This will help you on that nuclear fusion.*"

In 2010, a janitor was arrested for stealing boxes of personnel records, in connection with an identity theft ring[111]. In an earlier case, an identity theft ring relied on a janitor to steal personal information from patient files at a Chicago hospital. As many as 250 patients were possible victims of identity theft at Northwestern Memorial Hospital in the year-long identity scam, law enforcement authorities said.

---

[110] http://www.knoxnews.com/news/local/ex-janitor-gets-six-year-term-in-security-breach-ep-409915001-359351061.html

[111] http://www.databreachtoday.com/blogs/do-you-trust-your-janitor-p-715

Using the stolen information, the thieves obtained access to credit card data and charged more than $300,000 in more than 500 transactions to purchase jewelry, furniture, household goods, appliances and electronics. They then sold the items to friends and relatives for a cash profit. Some janitors have been discovered to have been doing this for *years* to hospitals[112],[113],[114]. The cleaning ladies have been caught stealing medical records as well[115]. In one case, the police found not only the clinic's property in the suspect's home, but also items from city hall and the library, as well as drugs. Protected health information in the paper records found included names, dates of birth, diagnostic codes, insurance information, patient account and medical chart numbers, and some Social Security numbers, according to the newspaper. The police also allege the employee stole unspecified equipment from the clinic.

---

[112] https://www.databreaches.net/former-ochsner-medical-center-janitor-pleads-guilty-to-stealing-patient-information/

[113] https://www.databreaches.net/hospital-janitor-and-girlfriend-charged-with-stealing-patients-identities/

[114] http://americanshredding.com/102/

[115] http://www.healthdatamanagement.com/news/clinic-cleaning-employee-stole-medical-records

How about the janitor the spent nearly *a year* stealing laptops from the business he worked at from 2011 to 2012[116]? According to sfexaminer.com, a janitor had been caught filching from Genentech. The medical company's computers were being stolen for nearly a year, from April 1, 2011 to February 5, 2012.

Approximately 30 laptop computers were stolen, the loss being estimated at $30,000. That is a big number but the amount is paltry compared to potential damages, such as the loss of corporate secrets (not that this appears to have been the case in this instance). This happened again recently to a school[117], where a former elementary school janitor plead guilty to stealing 30 laptop computers from the school and selling them online.

Bruce Wimmer writes in his book *'Business Espionage: Risks, Threats, and Countermeasures,'* the following story: "Another incident in Mexico involved a large international manufacturer of equipment and parts. This manufacturer operated a fairly sophisticated production facility. While much of the equipment was off-the-shelf equipment, the way it was configured and how it was used was a

---

[116]

http://www.alertboot.com/blog/blogs/endpoint_security/archive/2012/03/06/drive-encryption-software-janitor-steals-30-laptops-from-genentech.aspx

[117] http://www.washingtontimes.com/news/2016/jul/7/ex-janitor-get-year-in-jail-for-stealing-schools-l/

sensitive trade secret. The company took what they felt were reasonable precautions to protect their methodologies. One day, an engineer walking around the workshop did a double-take, because the janitor looked just like an individual with whom he went to university. He called out the man's name: 'Jorge, is that you? Hola!' The individual reacted but then tried to run away. Caught by security, the 'janitor' admitted that he was really an engineer and advised that he worked for a competitor. He told the security staff that he had been compelled by his employer to get hired as a janitor and spy. He regularly went back to the competitor company offices and advised them on what he observed, given the 'free reign' he had within the facility. Mexican staff that worked at the manufacturing company was surprised that an engineer would 'stoop' to working, even for a short time, as a janitor just to steal information. They were unaware of the business threat and the value of the information to a competitor.[118]"

Solutions

---

118

https://books.google.com/books?id=V9acBAAAQBAJ&pg=PA41&lpg=PA41&dq=janitor+china+steal&source=bl&ots=kuGdWR-eCr&sig=mjibPbXNfxUpbX5xc9Meg9p-Eko&hl=en&sa=X&ved=0ahUKEwj05IvWiJfOAhVH4oMKHUgaCZMQ6AEIHDAA#v=onepage&q=janitor%20china%20steal&f=false

It's clear that not only are the concerns for the myriad problems with cleaning, janitorial and contracted maintenance staff valid, they are actively being exploited. So, how can businesses protect themselves against this vulnerability?

First, insist that the contracted organization background check every employee, and include records from their country of origin, if they are not natively born. Any reputable company should already be doing this. They should also already be doing work eligibility verification, that is, an immigration status check. It is well worth asking to see proof that these tasks are actually happening, and insisting on seeing these records for the staff who will be servicing your business. It goes without saying, that the contracting company should also be licensed, bonded, and insured, as appropriate to their industry.

Second, every organization that is coming and servicing your business should be providing picture ID cards to their staff, and a work schedule to the security team. The cleaning crew should then be authenticated against this list, and confirmed to be known and expected individuals. Per some of the principles of security above, ensure that the workers only have physical access to areas they actually need to access.

Third, it may be a good idea to require a Business Associate Agreement from each contracting company. Primarily for medical companies, under the United States Health Insurance Portability and Accountability Act of 1996, a HIPAA business associate agreement (BAA) is a contract between a HIPAA covered entity and a HIPAA business associate (BA). The contract protects personal health information (PHI) in accordance with HIPAA guidelines[119].

The costs to implement these measures should be negligible, if one is already contracting with a reputable company. If they are contracting with a company not following these guidelines, switching to a more reputable vendor will certainly come with an increased cost, but these costs are nothing compared to a single incident or data breach. For those janitorial and cleaning companies who cannot or will not comply with these requirements, they would be facing a 'pivot or perish' moment. If there is a plethora of these companies going out of business, we may see an increase of these difficult to employ workers on the job market. I will not theorize on the possible political implications of this here.

Conclusions

---

[119] http://searchhealthit.techtarget.com/definition/HIPAA-business-associate-agreement-BAA

With all of this information in mind, it may still be a very slow process to start seeing wider adoption of these standards. An ever-frustrating axiom of the Information Security Principle is that there is always a trade-off between convenience and security. In the end, the security is only there to enable the business to be able to operate successfully. If the security protocols violate this rule, then the protocols with either be abolished or ignored. Additionally, many businesses will still opt to choose the least expensive service they find, and all too often, you get what you pay for. Compounding these issues with current mores regarding sensitivity to immigration and demographic status, I foresee that for the time being, unless there are further regulatory requirements, many businesses will simply turn a blind eye.

# Glossary

The following is a helpful glossary of common cybersecurity and Information Security-related terms, not all of which have been used in this book.

## A

### Access Control List

A list of credentials attached to a resource indicating whether or not the credentials have access to the resource. Also referred to as an ACL. ACL's are typically used for authorizing actions in applications.

### Active Attack

Any attack that involves actions that are detectable as an attack by the target. A port scan is active because it can be detected by the remote host. Of course it isn't really an attack. An active attack might involve posting data to an endpoint with the hope of achieving XSS or SQL Injection. Logging of regular http request/response activity that is later analyzed for potential vulnerabilities is passive.

### Advanced Encryption Standard (AES)

A fast, general-purpose block cipher standardized by NIST (the National Institute of Standards and Technology). The AES selection process was a multi-year competition, where Rijndael was the winning cipher.

### Anti-debugger

Referring to technology that detects or thwarts the use of a debugger on a piece of software.

### Anti-tampering

Referring to technology that attempts to thwart the reverse engineering and patching of a piece of software in binary format.

### Architectural security assessment

See also: Threat Model

### Asymmetric cryptography

Cryptography involving public keys, as opposed to cryptography making use of shared secrets.

See also: Symmetric cryptography.

### Audit

In the context of security, a review of a system in order to validate the security of the system. Generally, this either refers to code auditing or reviewing audit logs.

See also: Audit log, Code auditing.

### Audit log

Records that are kept for the purpose of later verifying that the security properties of a system have remained intact.

### Authenticate-and-encrypt

When using a cipher to encrypt and a MAC to provide message integrity, this paradigm specifies that one authenticates the plaintext and encrypts the plaintext, possibly in parallel. This is not secure in the general case.

See also: Authenticate-then-encrypt, Encrypt-then-authenticate.

### Authenticate-then-encrypt

When using a cipher to encrypt and a MAC to provide message integrity, this paradigm specifies that one authenticates the plaintext and then encrypts the plaintext concatenated with the MAC tag. This is not secure in the general case, but usually works well in practice.

See also: Authenticate-and-encrypt, Encrypt-then-authenticate.

## Authentication

The process of verifying that someone or something is the actual entity that they claim to be. Authentication is what happens when you log into a system. It compares your credentials (often user name and password) with a previously established known value such that the system can know that you are who you say you are. For sensitive systems, there is a trend toward using two factor authentication (2FA) which essentially means that users must supply two different secrets, usually one is a password (something they know) and the other is a pin supplied via text (verifying something they have).

## Authorization

Authorization is the process of determining whether an authenticated subject (a user) can see, change, delete or take other actions upon data. For example, if you log into a time keeping application, submit your timesheet and then your boss approves it, the act of logging in is authenticating, the act of filling out your timesheet and submitting should only be something your user is authorized to do and approving the timesheet is something only the boss is authorized to do. Authorization is tied to both #4 and #7 of the 2013 OWASP Top 10.

## B

## Backdoor

Malicious code inserted into a program for the purposes of providing the author covert access to machines running the program.

## Base 64

A method for encoding binary data into printable ASCII strings. Every byte of output maps to six bits of input (minus possible padding bytes).

**Big endian**

Refers to machines representing words most significant byte first. While x86 machines do not use big endian byte ordering (instead using little endian), the PowerPC and SPARC architectures do. This is also network byte order.

See also: Little endian.

**Birthday attack**

Take a function f() that seems to map an input to a random output of some fixed size (a pseudo-random function or PRF). A birthday attack is simply selecting random inputs for f() and checking to see if any previous values gave the same output. Statistically, if the output size is S bits, then one can find a collision in $2S/2$ operations, on average.

**Bit-flipping attack**

In a stream cipher, flipping a bit in the ciphertext flips the corresponding bit in the plaintext. If using a message authentication code (MAC), such attacks are not practical.

**Blacklist**

When performing input validation, the set of items that — if matched — result in the input being considered invalid. If no invalid items are found, the result is valid.

See also: Whitelist.

**Blinding**

A technique used to thwart timing attacks.

**Block cipher**

An encryption algorithm that maps inputs of size n to outputs of size n (n is called the block size). Data that is not a valid block size must somehow be padded (generally by using an encryption mode). The same input always produces the same output.

See also: Stream cipher.

**Blowfish**

A block cipher with 64-bit blocks and variable length keys, created by Bruce Schneier. This cipher is infamous for having slow key-setup times.

**Brute-force attack**

An attack on an encryption algorithm where the encryption key for a ciphertext is determined by trying to decrypt with every key until valid plaintext is obtained.

**Buffer overflow**

A buffer overflow is when you can put more data into a memory location than is allocated to hold that data. Languages like C and C++ that do no built-in bounds checking are susceptible to such problems. These problems are often security-critical.

**C**

**CA**

See also: Certification Authority.

**Canary**

A piece of data, the absence of which indicates a violation of a security policy. Several tools use a canary for preventing certain stack-smashing buffer overflow attacks.

See also: Buffer overflow, Stack smashing.

### Capture-replay attacks

When an attacker can capture data off the wire and replay it later without the bogus data being detected as bogus.

### Certificate

A data object that binds information about a person or some other entity to a public key. The binding is generally done using a digital signature from a trusted third party (a certification authority).

### Certificate Revocation List

A list published by a certification authority indicating which issued certificates should be considered invalid.

### Certificate Signing Request

Data about an entity given to a certification authority. The authority will package the data into a certificate and sign the certificate if the data in the signing request is validated.

### Certification Authority

An entity that manages digital certificates — i.e., issues and revokes. Verisign and InstantSSL are two well-known CAs.

### Chain responder

An OCSP responder that relays the results of querying another OCSP responder.

See also: OCSP.

### Choke point

In computer security, a place in a system where input is routed for the purposes of performing data validation. The implication is that there are few such places in a system and that all data must pass through one or more of the choke points. The idea is that funneling input through a small number of choke points makes it easier to ensure that input is properly validated. One potential concern is that poorly chosen choke points may not have enough information to perform input validation that is as accurate as possible.

### chroot

A UNIX system call that sets the root directory for a process to any arbitrary directory. The idea is compartmentalization: Even if a process is compromised, it should not be able to see interesting parts of the file system beyond its own little world. There are some instances where chroot "jails" can be circumvented; it can be difficult to build proper operating environments to make chroot work well.

### Cipher-Block Chaining mode

A block cipher mode that provides secrecy but not message integrity. Messages encrypted with this mode should have random initialization vectors.

### Cipher Feedback mode

A mode that turns a block cipher into a stream cipher. This mode is safe only when used in particular configurations. Generally, CTR mode and OFB mode are used instead since both have better security bounds.

### Ciphertext

The result of encrypting a message.

See also: Plaintext.

### Ciphertext stealing mode

A block cipher mode of operation that is similar to CBC mode except that the final block is processed in such a way that the output is always the same length as the input. That is, this mode is similar to CBC mode but does not require padding.

See also: Cipher-Block Chaining mode, Padding.

**Code auditing**

Reviewing computer software for security problems.

See also: Audit.

**Code signing**

Signing executable code to establish that it comes from a trustworthy vendor. The signature must be validated using a trusted third party in order to establish identity.

**Compartmentalization**

Separating a system into parts with distinct boundaries, using simple, well- defined interfaces. The basic idea is that of containment — i.e., if one part is compromised, perhaps the extent of the damage can be limited.

See also: Jail, Chroot.

**Comprehesive, Lightweight Application Security Process**

An activity-driven, role-based set of process components whose core contains formalized best practices for building security into your existing or new-start software development lifecycles in a structured, repeatable, and measurable way.

**Context object**

In a cryptographic library, a data object that holds the intermediate state associated with the cryptographic processing of a piece of data. For example, if incrementally hashing a string, a context object stores the internal state of the hash function necessary to process further data.

## CRAM

A password-based authentication mechanism using a cryptographic hash function (usually MD5). It does not provide adequate protection against several common threats to password-based authentication systems. HTTP Digest Authentication is a somewhat better alternative; it is replacing CRAM in most places.

## CRC

Cyclic Redundancy Check. A means of determining whether accidental transmission errors have occurred. Such algorithms are not cryptographically secure because attackers can often forge CRC values or even modify data maliciously in such a way that the CRC value does not change. Instead, one should use a strong, keyed message authentication code such as HMAC or OMAC.

See also: HMAC, Message Authentication Code, OMAC.

## Critical extensions

In an X.509 certificate, those extensions that must be recognized by any software processing the certificate. If a piece of software does not recognize an extension marked as critical, the software must regard the certificate as invalid.

## CRL

See also: Certificate Revocation List.

## Cross-site request forgery

CSRF is an attack which forces an end user to execute unwanted actions on a web application in which he/she is currently authenticated. With little help of social engineering (like sending a link via email/chat), an attacker may force the users of a web application to execute actions of the attackers choosing. A successful CSRF exploit can compromise end user data and operation in case of normal user. If the targeted end user is the administrator account, this can compromise the entire web application.

**Cross-site scripting**

A class of problems resulting from insufficient input validation where one user can add content to a web site that can be malicious when viewed by other users to the web site. For example, one might post to a message board that accepts arbitrary HTML and include a malicious code item.

**Cryptanalysis**

The science of breaking cryptographic algorithms.

**Cryptographic hash function**

A function that takes an input string of arbitrary length and produces a fixed- size output — where it is unfeasible to find two inputs that map to the same output, and it is unfeasible to learn anything about the input from the output.

**Cryptographic randomness**

Data produced by a cryptographic pseudo-random number generator. The probability of figuring out the internal state of the generator is related to the strength of the underlying cryptography — i.e., assuming the generator is seeded with enough entropy.

**Cryptography**

The science of providing secrecy, integrity, and non-repudiation for data.

**CSR**

See also: Certificate Signing Request.

**CSS**

Cross-site scripting. Generally, however, this is abbreviated to XSS in order to avoid confusion with cascading style sheets.

See also: Cross-site scripting.

**CTR mode**

See also: Counter mode.

**CWC mode**

See also: Carter Wegmen + Counter mode.

**D**

**DACL**

Discretionary Access Control List. In a Windows ACL, a list that determines access rights to an object.

See also: Access Control List.

**Davies-Meyer**

An algorithm for turning a block cipher into a cryptographic one-way hash function.

**Default deny**

A paradigm for access control and input validation where an action must explicitly be allowed. The idea behind this paradigm is that one should limit the possibilities for unexpected behavior by being strict, instead of lenient, with rules.

**Defense-in-depth**

A principle for building systems stating that multiple defensive mechanisms at different layers of a system are usually more secure than a single layer of defense. For example, when performing input validation, one might validate user data as it comes in and then also validate it before each use — just in case something was not caught, or the underlying components are linked against a different front end, etc.

### DEK

Data encrypting key.

### Delta CRLs

A variation of Certificate Revocation Lists that allows for incremental updating, as an effort to avoid frequently re-downloading a large amount of unchanged data.

See also: Certificate Revocation List.

### Denial of service attack

Any attack that affects the availability of a service. Reliability bugs that cause a service to crash or go into some sort of vegetative state are usually potential denial-of-service problems.

### DES

See also: Data Encryption Standard, Triple DES.

### DESX

An extended version of DES that increases the resistance to brute-force attack in a highly efficient way by increasing the key length. The extra key material is mixed into the encryption process, using XORs. This technique does not improve resistance to differential attacks, but such attacks are still generally considered unfeasible against DES.

See also: DES.

## Dictionary attack

An attack against a cryptographic system, using precomputating values to build a dictionary. For example, in a password system, one might keep a dictionary mapping ciphertext pairs in plaintext form to keys for a single plaintext that frequently occurs. A large enough key space can render this attack useless. In a password system, there are similar dictionary attacks, which are somewhat alleviated by salt. The end result is that the attacker — once he knows the salt — can do a "Crack"-style dictionary attack. Crack-style attacks can be avoided to some degree by making the password verifier computationally expensive to compute. Or select strong random passwords, or do not use a password-based system.

## Differential cryptanalysis

A type of cryptographic attack where an attacker who can select related inputs learns information about the key from comparing the outputs. Modern ciphers of merit are designed in such a way as to thwart such attacks. Also note that such attacks generally require enough chosen plaintexts as to be considered unfeasible, even when there is a cipher that theoretically falls prey to such a problem.

## Diffie-Hellman key exchange

A method for exchanging a secret key over an untrusted medium in such a way as to preserve the secrecy of the key. The two parties both contribute random data that factors into the final shared secret. The fundamental problem with this method is authenticating the party with whom you exchanged keys. The simple Diffie-Hellman protocol does not do that. One must also use some public-key authentication system such as DSA.

See also: DSA, Station-to-station protocol.

## Digest size

The output size for a hash function.

**Data Encryption Standard**

An encryption algorithm standardized by the US Government. The key length is too short, so this algorithm should be considered insecure. The effective key strength is 56 bits; the actual key size is 64 bits — 8 bits are wasted. However, there are variations such as Triple DES and DESX that increase security while also increasing the key size.

See also: Advanced Encryption Standard, Triple DES.

**Digital signature**

Data that proves that a document (or other piece of data) was not modified since being processed by a particular entity. Generally, what this really means is that — if someone 'signs' a piece of data — anyone who has the right public key can demonstrated which private key was used to sign the data.

**Digital Signature Algorithm**

See also: DSA.

**Distinguished Encoding Rules**

A set of rules used that describes how to encode ASN.1 data objects unambiguously.

See also: ASN.1.

**Distinguished Name**

In an X.509 certificate, a field that uniquely specifies the user or group to which the certificate is bound. Usually, the Distinguished Name will contain a user's name or User ID, an organizational name, and a country designation. For a server certificate, it will often contain the DNS name of the machine.

**DN**

See also: Distinguished Name.

**DoS**

Denial of Service.

See also: Denial of service attack.

**DSA**

The Digital Signature Algorithm, a public key algorithm dedicated to digital signatures which was standardized by NIST. It is based on the same mathematical principles as Diffie-Hellman.

**E**

**Eavesdropping attack**

Any attack on a data connection where one simply records or views data instead of tampering with the connection.

See also: Passive attack.

**ECB Mode**

See also: Electronic Code Book mode.

**ECC**

See also: Eliptic Curve Cryptography.

**EGD**

See also: Entropy Gathering Daemon.

**Electronic Code Book mode**

An encryption mode for block ciphers that is more or less a direct use of the underlying block cipher. The only difference is that a message is padded out to a multiple of the block length. This mode should not be used under any circumstances.

### Eliptic Curve Cryptography

A type of public key cryptography that — due to smaller key sizes — tends to be more efficient that standard cryptography. The basic algorithms are essentially the same, except that the operations are performed over different mathematical groups (called eliptic curves).

### EME-OAEP padding

A padding scheme for public key cryptography that uses a "random" value generated, using a cryptographic hash function in order to prevent particular types of attacks against RSA.

See also: PKCS #1 padding.

### Envelope Encryption

Also known as Key Wrapping.

A method of encrypting data/key using DEK (Data Encryption Key) which is then encrypted with the MEK (Master Encryption Key) or KEK (Key Encryption Key). In some uses, only the KEK is used and MEK is not used.

### Encrypt-then-authenticate

When using a cipher to encrypt and a MAC to provide message integrity, this paradigm specifies that one encrypts the plaintext, then MACs the ciphertext. This paradigm has theoretically appealing properties and is recommended to use in practice.

See also: Authenticate-and-encrypt, Authenticate-then-encrypt.

### Endianess

The byte ordering scheme that a machine uses (usually either little endian or big endian).

See also:Big endian, Little endian.

## Entropy

Refers to the inherent unknowability of data to external observers. If a bit is just as likely to be a 1 as a 0 and a user does not know which it is, then the bit contains one bit of entropy.

## Entropy Gathering Daemon

A substitute for /dev/random; a tool used for entropy harvesting.

## Entropy harvester

A piece of software responsible for gathering entropy from a machine and distilling it into small pieces of high entropy data. Often an entropy harvester will produce a seed for a cryptographic pseudo-random number generator.

See also: Entropy, Pseudo-random number generator.

## Ephemeral keying

Using one-time public key pairs for session key exchange in order to prevent recovering previous session keys if a private key is compromised. Long-term public key pairs are still used to establish identity.

## Euclidian algorithm

An algorithm that computes the greatest common divisor of any two numbers.

## Extended Euclidian algorithm

An algorithm used to compute the inverse of a number modulo "some other number."

## F

**Fingerprint**

The output of a cryptographic hash function.

See also: Message digest.

**FIPS**

Federal Information Processing Standard; a set of standards from NIST.

**FIPS-140**

A standard authored by the U.S. National Institute of Standards and Technology, that details general security requirements for cryptographic software deployed in a government systems (primarily cryptographic providers).

See also: NIST, FIPS.

**Format string attack**

The C standard library uses specifiers to format output. If an attacker can control the input to such a format string, he can often write to arbitrary memory locations.

**Forward secrecy**

Ensuring that the compromise of a secret does not divulge information that could lead to data protected prior to the compromise. In many systems with forward secrecy, it is only provided on a per-session basis, meaning that a key compromise will not affect previous sessions, but would allow an attacker to decrypt previous messages sent as a part of the current session.

See also: Perfect forward secrecy.

**G**

**H**

**Hash function**

A function that maps a string of arbitrary length to a fixed size value in a deterministic manner. Such a function may or may not have cryptographic applications.

See also: Cryptographic hash function, Universal hash function, One-way hash function.

**Hash function (cryptographic)**

See also: Cryptographic hash function.

**Hash function (one-way)**

See also: One-way hash function.

**Hash function (universal)**

See also: Universal hash function.

**Hash output**

See also: Hash value.

**Hash value**

The output of a hash function.

See also: Fingerprint, Message digest.

**HMAC**

A well-known algorithm for converting a cryptographic one-way hash function into a message authentication code.

**Honey Pot**

A strategy of setting up resources which an attacker believes are real but are infact designed specifically to catch the attacker.

**I**

**IDEA**

A block cipher with 128-bit keys and 64-bit blocks popularly used with PGP. It is currently protected by patents.

**Identity establishment**

See Authentication

**Impact**

A component of Risk, the impact describes the negative effect that results from a risk being realised. Example impacts include financial loss, legal and regulatory issues, brand and reputation damage, data loss, breach of contract, and so on. Impacts can be reduced as part of risk mitigation. For example, installing a second hard drive and configuring it as a RAID mirror of a primary hard drive reduces the impact of a disk failure. It does not address the likelihood of a disk failure at all.

Impacts, like risks, can be technical or business related. For example, a technical impact could be corrupt data in the table storing a firm's outstanding orders. The business impact might be customer ill-will, increased customer service costs, and additional costs shipping and tracking replacement items.

Some impacts can be contractually transferred to another party. Insurance, for example, can transfer the financial impact of a business risk to the insurer in exchange for a premium payment by the insured. The technical impact of a DDoS attack can be transferred to another entity by using their network and server resources. Not all impacts can be transferred. Brand and reputation damage, some legal and regulatory liability, and impacts on business qualities like time-to-market cannot be transferred.

**Indirect CRLs**

A CRL issued by a third party, that can contain certificates from multiple CA's.

See also: Certificate, Certificate Revocation List, Certification Authority.

### Initialization vector

A value used to initialize a cryptographic algorithm. Often, the implication is that the value must be random.

See also: Nonce, Salt.

### Input validation

The act of determining that data input to a program is sound.

### Integer overflow

When an integer value is too big to be held by its associated data type, the results can often be disastrous. This is often a problem when converting unsigned numbers to signed values.

### Integrity checking

The act of checking whether a message has been modified either maliciously or by accident. Cryptographically strong message integrity algorithms should always be used when integrity is important.

### Interleaved encryption

Processing the encryption of a message as multiple messages, generally treating every nth block as part of a single message.

### ISO/IEC 17799

Provides best practice recommendations on information security management for use by those who are responsible for initiating, implementing or maintaining information security management systems.

**IV**

See also: Initialization vector.

**J**

**Jail**

A restricted execution environment meant to compartmentalize a process, so that — even if it has security problems — it cannot hurt resources which it would not normally have access to use. On FreeBSD, a system call similar to chroot that provides compartmentalization. Unlike chroot, it can also restrict network resources in addition to file system resources.

See also: chroot.

**K**

**Kerberos**

An authentication protocol that relies solely on symmetric cryptography, as opposed to public key cryptography. It still relies on a trusted third party (an authentication server). While Kerberos is often looked upon as a way to avoid problems with Public Key Infrastructure, it can be difficult to scale Kerberos beyond medium-sized organizations.

See also: Public Key Infrastructure, Trusted third party.

**Key agreement**

The process of two parties agreeing on a shared secret, where both parties contribute material to the key.

**Key establishment**

The process of agreeing on a shared secret, where both parties contribute material to the key.

**Key exchange**

The process of two parties agreeing on a shared secret, usually implying that both parties contribute to the key.

**Key management**

Mechanisms and process for secure creation, storage, and handling of key material.

**Key schedule**

In a block cipher, keys used for individual "rounds" of encryption, derived from the base key in a cipher-dependent manner.

**Key transport**

When one party picks a session key and communicates it to a second party.

**Keystream Output**

from a stream cipher.

See also: Pseudo-random number generator, Stream cipher.

**L**

**LDAP**

Lightweight Directory Access Protocol. A directory protocol commonly used for storing and distributing CRLs.

**Length extension attack**

A class of attack on message authentication codes, where a tag can be forged without the key by extending a pre-existing message in a particular way. CBC-MAC in its simplest form has this problem, but variants protect against it (particularly OMAC).

See also: Message Authentication Code, OMAC.

## Likelihood

A component of risk, likelihood describes the chance that a risk will be realised and the negative impact will occur. It is typically described in general terms like "low," "medium," and "high". Sometimes an actual probability is possible (e.g., the probability of two documents producing the same CRC-16 is approximately 1 in 65536).

The likelihood of a technical risk is often related to the likelihood of a vulnerability being successfully exploited. This likelihood is often influenced by factors like how accessible the vulnerability is, the degree to which special tools need to be used to be successful, the amount of specialised knowledge an attacker needs, and so on.

Likelihood is combined with impact to produce a severity estimate for a risk.

## LFSR

See also: Linear Feedback Shift Register.

## Linear cryptanalysis

A type of cryptanalytic attack where linear approximations of behavior are used. Modern ciphers of merit are designed in such a way as to thwart such attacks. Also note that such attacks generally require enough chosen plaintexts as to be considered unfeasible — even when there is a cipher that theoretically falls prey to such a problem (such as DES).

## Linear Feedback Shift Register

A non-cryptographic class of pseudo-random number generators, where output is determined by shifting out "output" bits and shifting in "input" bits, where the input bits are a function of the internal state of the register, perhaps combined with new entropy. LFSRs are based on polynomial math, and are not secure in and of themselves; however, they can be put to good use as a component in more secure cryptosystems.

## Little endian

Refers to machines representing words of data least significant byte first, such as the Intel x86.

See also: Big endian.

## M

## MAC

See also: Message Authentication Code.

## Man-in-the-middle attack

An eavesdropping attack where a client's communication with a server is proxied by an attacker. Generally, the implication is that the client performs a cryptographic key exchange with an entity and fails to authenticate that entity, thus allowing an attacker to look like a valid server.

## Matyas-Meyer-Oseas

A construction for turning a block cipher into a cryptographic one-way hash function.

## MCF

The Modular Crypt Format, a de-facto data format standard for storing password hashes commonly used on UNIX boxes as a replacement for the traditional UNIX crypt() format.

## MD-strengthening

Merkel-Damgard strengthening, a general method for turning a collision- resistant compression function into a collision-resistant hash function by adding padding and an encoded length to the end of the input message. The key point behind MD-strengthening is that no possible input to the underlying hash function can be the tail end of a different input.

### MD2

A cryptographic hash function optimized for 16-bit platforms. It has poor performance characteristics on other platforms and has a weak internal structure.

### MD4

A cryptographic hash function that is known to be broken and should not be used under any circumstances.

### MD5

A popular and fast cryptographic hash function that outputs 128-bit message digests. Its internal structure is known to be weak and should be avoided if at all possible.

### MD5-MCF

A way of using MD5 to store password authentication information, using the modular crypt format.

See also: MCF, MD5.

### MDC2

A construction for turning a block cipher into a cryptographic hash function, where the output length is twice the block size of the cipher.

### Meet-in-the-middle attack

A theoretical attack against encrypting a message twice using a single block cipher and two different keys. For example, double encryption with DES theoretically is no more secure than DES, which is why Triple DES became popular (it gives twice the effective key strength).

**Message Authentication Code**

A function that takes a message and a secret key (and possibly a nonce) and produces an output that cannot, in practice, be forged without possessing the secret key.

**Message digest**

The output of a hash function.

**Message integrity**

A message has integrity if it maintains the value it is supposed to maintain, as opposed to being modified on accident or as part of an attack.

**Methodology**

A mature set of processes applied to various stages of an applications' lifecycle to help reduce the likelihood of security vulnerabilities presence or exploitation.

**Metrics**

A metric is a standard unit of measure, such as meter or mile for length, or gram or ton for weight, or more generally, part of a system of parameters, or systems of measurement, or a set of ways of quantitatively and periodically measuring, assessing, controlling or selecting a person, process, event, or institution, along with the procedures to carry out measurements and the procedures for the interpretation of the assessment in the light of previous or comparable assessments.

## Miller-Rabin

A primality test that is efficient because it is probabilistic, meaning that there is some chance it reports a composite (non-prime) number as a prime. There is a trade-off between efficiency and probability, but one can gain extremely high assurance without making unreasonable sacrifices in efficiency.

## Model

A model is a pattern, plan, representation (especially in miniature), or description designed to show the main object or workings of an object, system, or concept.

## Modulus

In the context of public key cryptography, a value by which all other values are reduced. That is, if a number is bigger than the modulus, the value of the number is considered to be the same as if the number were the remainder after dividing the number by the modulus.

## N

## Near-collision resistance

Given a plaintext value and the corresponding hash value, it should be computationally unfeasible to find a second plaintext value that gives the same hash value.

## NIST

The National Institute of Standards and Technology is a division of the U.S. Department of Commerce. NIST issues standards and guidelines, with the hope that they will be adopted by the computing community.

## Non-repudiation

The capability of establishing that a message was signed by a particular entity. That is, a message is said to be non-repudiatable when a user sends it, and one can prove that the user sent it. In practice, cryptography can demonstrate that only particular key material was used to produce a message. There are always legal defenses such as stolen credentials or duress.

## Nonce

A value used with a cryptographic algorithm that must be unique in order to maintain the security of the system. Generally, the uniqueness requirement holds only for a single key — meaning that a {key, nonce} pair should never be reused.

See also: Initialization vector, Salt.

## O

## OCB mode

See also: Offset Code Book mode.

## OCSP

See also: Online Certificate Status Protocol.

## OCSP responder

The server side software that answers OCSP requests.

See also: Online Certificate Status Protocol.

## OFB mode

See also: Output Feedback mode.

## Offset Code Book mode

A patented encryption mode for block ciphers that provides both secrecy and message integrity and is capable of doing so at high speeds.

**OMAC**

One-key CBC-MAC. A secure, efficient way for turning a block cipher into a message authentication code. It is an improvement of the CBC-MAC, which is not secure in the arbitrary case. Other CBC-MAC variants use multiple keys in order to fix the problem with CBC-MAC. OMAC uses a single key and still has appealing provable security properties.

**One-time pad**

A particular cryptographic system that is provably secure in some sense, but highly impractical, because it requires a bit of entropy for every bit of message.

**One-time password**

A password that is only valid once. Generally, such passwords are derived from some master secret — which is shared by an entity and an authentication server — and are calculated via a challenge-response protocol.

**One-way hash function**

A hash function, where it is computationally unfeasible to determine anything about the input from the output.

**Online Certificate Status Protocol**

A protocol for determining whether a digital certificate is valid in real time without using CRLs. This protocol (usually abbreviated OCSP) is specified in RFC 2560.

**Output Feedback mode**

A block cipher mode that turns a block cipher into a stream cipher. The mode works by continually encrypting the previous block of keystream. The first block of keystream is generated by encrypting an initialization vector.

**P**

## Padding

Data added to a message that is not part of the message. For example, some block cipher modes require messages to be padded to a length that is evenly divisible by the block length of the cipher — i.e., the number of bytes that the cipher processes at once.

## PAM

Pluggable Authentication Modules is a technology for abstracting out authentication at the host level. It is similar to SASL, but is a bit higher up in the network stack and tends to be a much easier technology to use, particularly for system administrators, who can configure authentication policies quite easily using PAM.

See also: SASL.

## Partial collision resistance

When it is unfeasible to find two arbitrary inputs to a hash function that produce similar outputs — i.e., outputs that differ in only a few bits.

## Passive attack

See also: Eavesdropping attack.

## Passphrase

A synonym for "password," meant to encourage people to use longer (it is hoped, more secure) values.

## Password

A value that is used for authentication.

## PBKDF2

Password-Based Key Derivation Function #2. An algorithm defined in PKCS #5 for deriving a random value from a password.

**PEM encoding**

A simple encoding scheme for cryptographic objects that outputs printable values (by Base 64 encoding a DER-encoded representation of the cryptographic object). The scheme was first introduced in Privacy Enhanced Mail, a defunct way of providing E-mail security.

**Perfect forward secrecy**

Ensuring that the compromise of a secret does not divulge information that could lead to the recovery of data protected prior to the compromise.

See also: Forward secrecy.

**PKI**

See also: Public Key Infrastructure.

**Plaintext**

An unencrypted message.

See also: Ciphertext.

**PMAC**

The MAC portion of the OCB block cipher mode. It is a patented way of turning a block cipher into a secure, parallelizable MAC.

**Precomputation attack**

Any attack that involves precomputing significant amounts of data in advance of opportunities to launch an attack. A dictionary attack is a common precomputation attack.

**Predictive modelling**

Predictive modelling is the process by which a model is created or chosen to try to best predict the probability of an outcome. In many cases the model is chosen on the basis of detection theory to try to guess the probability of a signal given a set amount of input data, for example given an email determining how likely that it is spam.

**Private key**

In a public key cryptosystem, key material that is bound tightly to an individual entity that must remain secret in order for there to be secure communication.

**Privilege separation**

A technique for trying to minimize the impact that a programming flaw can have, where operations requiring privilege are separated out into a small, independent component (hopefully audited with care). Generally, the component is implemented as an independent process, and it spawns off a non-privileged process to do most of the real work. The two processes keep open a communication link, speaking a simple protocol.

**PRNG**

See also: Pseudo-random number generator.

**Pseudo-random number generator**

An algorithm that produces statistically random outputs. Many PRNGs are completely predictable, though their outputs are statistically random. A pseudo-random number generator may be operated in a secure way if it is regularly "seeded" with enough unpredictable entropy. Most popular pseudo-random number generators are not secure.

See also: Stream cipher and #Entropy.

## Public key

In a public key cryptosystem, the key material that can be published publicly without compromising the security of the system. Generally, this material must be published; its authenticity must be determined definitively.

## Public Key Infrastructure

A system that provides a means for establishing trust as to what identity is associated with a public key. Some sort of Public Key Infrastructure (PKI) is necessary to give reasonable assurance that one is communicating securely with the proper party, even if that infrastructure is ad hoc"

## Q

### QRLJacking

QRLJacking or Quick Response Code Login Jacking is a simple social engineering attack vector capable of session hijacking affecting all applications that rely on "Login with QR code" feature as a secure way to login into accounts. In a simple way, In a nutshell victim scans the attacker's QR code results of session hijacking.

## R

### RA

See also: Registration Authority.

### Race condition

A class of error in environments that are multi-threaded or otherwise multi- tasking, where an operation is falsely assumed to be atomic. That is, if two operations overlap instead of being done sequentially, there is some risk of the resulting computation not being correct. There are many cases where such a condition can be security critical.

See also: TOCTOU problem.

## Randomness

Randomness has both mathematical and colloquial definitions. Mathematically speaking, *random* outcomes are independent and equally likely to occur. Colloquially, *random* usually implies being unpredictable and/or unguessable. Random data is often tested with statistical tests that search for evidence to disprove the assertion that the data is random (e.g., patterns, cycles, bias). Data that is statistically random can be completely predictable. Thus it is usually insufficient to refer to "random data".

See also: Entropy.

## RC2

A block cipher with variable key sizes and 64-bit blocks.

## RC4

A widely used stream cipher that is relatively fast but with some significant problems. One practical problem is that it has a weak key setup algorithm, though this problem can be mitigated with care. Another more theoretical problem is that RC4's output is easy to distinguish from a truly random stream of numbers. This problem indicates that RC4 is probably not a good long-term choice for data security.

## RC5

A block cipher that has several tunable parameters.

## Registration Authority

An organization that is responsible for validating the identity of entities trying to obtain credentials in a Public Key Infrastructure.

See also: Certification Authority, Public Key Infrastructure.

## Rekeying

Changing a key in a cryptographic system.

## Related key attack

A class of cryptographic attack where one takes advantage of known relationships between keys to expose information about the keys or the messages those keys are protecting.

## Revocation

In the context of Public Key Infrastructure, the act of voiding a digital certificate.

See also: X.509 certificate.

## Risk

Risk is the possibility of a negative or undesirable occurance. There are two independent parts of risk: Impact and Likelihood. To reduce risk, one can reduce the impact, reduce the likelihood, or both. Risk can also be accepted (meaning that the full impact of the negative outcome will be borne by the entity at risk). The impact and likelihood of a risk are usually combined to create an estimate of its Severity.

## RIPEMD-160

A cryptographic hash function that is well regarded. It has a 160-bit output, and is a bit slower than SHA1.

## RMAC

A construction for making a Message Authentication Code out of a block cipher. It is not generally secure in the way that OMAC is, and is generally considered not worth using due to the existence of better alternatives.

See also: OMAC.

## Rollback attack

An attack where one forces communicating parties to agree on an insecure protocol version.

## Root certificate

A certificate that is intrinsically trusted by entities in a Public Key Infrastructure — generally should be transported over a secure medium. Root certificates belong to a Certification Authority and are used to sign other certificates that are deemed to be valid. When a system tries to establish the validity of a certificate, one of the first things that should happen is that it should look for a chain of trust to a known, trusted root certificate. That is, if the certificate to be validated is not signed by a root, one checks the certificate(s) used to sign it to determine if those were signed by a root cert. Lather, rinse, repeat.

See also: Public Key Infrastructure.

## Round

In a block cipher, a group of operations applied as a unit that has an inverse that undoes the operation. Most block ciphers define a round operation and then apply that round operation numerous times — though often applying a different key for each round, where the round key is somehow derived from the base key.

## RSA

A popular public key algorithm for encryption and digital signatures invented by Ron Rivest, Adi Shamir and Leonard Adleman. It is believed that, if factoring large numbers is computationally unfeasible, then RSA can be used securely in practice.

## RSASSA-PSS

A padding standard defined in PKCS #1, used for padding data prior to RSA signing operations.

## S

### S/Key

A popular One-time password system.

### S/MIME

A protocol for secure electronic mail standardized by the IETF. It relies on standard X.509-based Public Key Infrastructure.

### SACL

System Access Control List. In Windows, the part of an ACL that determines audit logging policy.

See also: Access Control List, DACL.

### Salt

Data that can be public but is used to prevent against precomputation attacks.

See also: Initialization vector, Nonce.

### SASL

The Simple Authentication and Security Layer, which is a method for adding authentication services to network protocols somewhat generically. It is also capable of providing key exchange in many circumstances.

### Secret key

See also: Symmetric key.

### Secure Socket Layer

A popular protocol for establishing secure channels over a reliable transport, utilizing a standard X.509 Public Key Infrastructure for authenticating machines. This protocol has evolved into the TLS protocol, but the term SSL is often used to generically refer to both.

See also: Transport Layer Security.

**SEED**

128-bit Symmetric Block Cipher

**Seed**

A value used to initialize a pseudo-random number generator.

See also: Entropy, Initialization vector, Pseudo-random number generator.

**Self-signed certificate**

A certificate signed by the private key associated with that certificate. In an X.509 Public Key Infrastructure, all certificates need to be signed. Since root certificates have no third-party signature to establish their authenticity, they are used to sign themselves. In such a case, trust in the certificate must be established by some other means.

**Serpent**

A modern block cipher with 128-bit blocks and variable-sized keys. A finalist in the AES competition, Serpent has a higher security margin by design than other candidates, and is a bit slower on typical 32-bit hardware as a result.

See also: AES.

**Session Token**

A value that represents a user's identity during their session. Typically the user provides some form of credentials (e.g., username, password, possibly a one-time token value from a second authentication factor) and the server returns a token value that represents the user's identity. In web applications, this token is often returned in a cookie. The client application includes the session token with each request, enabling the server to associate each request with the same user, role, and session.

**Severity**

The severity of a risk combines its likelihood and impact into a single measure. This combination often follows the guidance of NIST Special Publication 800-30, though some practitioners opt to use their own scale.

|  | | Impact | | |
|---|---|---|---|---|
|  | | **Low** | **Medium** | **High** |
|  | **High** | Low | Medium | High |
| **Likelihood** | **Medium** | Low | Medium | Medium |
|  | **Low** | Low | Low | Low |

**SHA-256**

A cryptographic hash function from NIST with 256-bit message digests.

**SHA-384**

SHA-512 with a truncated digest (as specified by NIST).

**SHA-512**

A cryptographic hash function from NIST with 512-bit message digests.

**SHA1**

A fairly fast, well regarded hash function with 160-bit digests that has been standardized by the National Institute of Standards and Technology (NIST).

**Shared secret**

A value shared by parties that may wish to communicate, where the secrecy of that value is an important component of secure communications. Typically, a shared secret is either an encryption key, a MAC key, or some value used to derive such keys.

See also: Symmetric key.

**Shatter attack**

A class of attack on the Windows event system. The Windows messaging system is fundamentally fragile from a security perspective because it allows for arbitrary processes to insert control events into the message queue without sufficient mechanisms for authentication. Sometimes messages can be used to trick other applications to execute malicious code.

**SIEM**

In the field of computer security, security information and event management (SIEM), software products and services combine security information management (SIM) and security event management (SEM). They provide real-time analysis of security alerts generated by applications and network hardware.

**Single sign-on**

Single sign-on allows you to access all computing resources that you should be able to reach by using a single set of authentication credentials that are presented a single time per login session. Single sign-on is a notion for improved usability of security systems that can often increase the security exposure of a system significantly.

### Snooping attacks

Attacks where data is read off a network while in transit without modifying or destroying the data.

### SNOW

A very fast stream cipher that is patent-free and seems to have a very high security margin.

### SQL Injection

SQL injection is a security vulnerability that occurs in the persistence/database layer of a web application. This vulnerability is derived from the incorrect escaping of variables embedded in SQL statements. It is in fact an instance of a more general class of vulnerabilities based on poor input validation and bad design that can occur whenever one programming or scripting language is embedded inside another.

### SSL

See also: Secure Socket Layer.

### Stack smashing

Overwriting a return address on the program execution stack by exploiting a buffer overflow. Generally, the implication is that the return address gets replaced with a pointer to malicious code.

See also: Buffer overflow.

### Station-to-station protocol

A simple variant of the Diffie-Hellman key exchange protocol that provides key agreement and authenticates each party to the other. This is done by adding digital signatures (which must be done carefully).

See also: Diffie-Hellman key exchange.

**Stream cipher**

A pseudo-random number generator that is believed to be cryptographically strong and always produces the same stream of output given the same initial seed (i.e., key). Encrypting with a stream cipher consists of combining the plaintext with the keystream, usually via XOR.

See also: Pseudo-random number generator, Block cipher.

**Strong collision resistance**

Strong collision resistance is a property that a hash function may have (and a good cryptographic hash function will have), characterized by it being computationally unfeasible to find two arbitrary inputs that yield the same output.

See also: Hash function, Weak collision resistance.

**Surreptitious forwarding**

An attack on some public key cryptosystems where a malicious user decrypts a digitally signed message and then encrypts the message using someone else's public key: giving the end receiver the impression that the message was originally destined for them.

**Symmetric cryptography**

Cryptography that makes use of shared secrets as opposed to public keys.

**Symmetric key**

See also: Shared secret.

**T**

**Tag**

The result of applying a keyed message authentication code to a message.

See also: Message Authentication Code.

**Tamper-proofing**

See also: Anti-tampering.

**Threat model**

A representation of the system threats that are expected to be reasonable. This includes denoting what kind of resources an attacker is expected to have, in addition to what kinds of things the attacker may be willing to try to do. Sometimes called an architectural security assessment.

See also: OWASP Threat Model Project

**Time of check, time of use problem**

See also: TOCTOU problem.

**TMAC**

A two-keyed variant of the CBC-MAC that overcomes the fundamental limitation of that MAC.

See also: Message Authentication Code, CBC-MAC, OMAC.

**TOCTOU problem**

Time-of-check, time-of-use race condition. A type of race condition between multiple processes on a file system. Generally what happens is that a single program checks some sort of property on a file, and then in subsequent instructions tries to use the resource if the check succeeded. The problem is that — even if the use comes immediately after the check — there is often some significant chance that a second process can invalidate the check in a malicious way. For example, a privileged program might check write privileges on a valid file, and the attacker can then replace that file with a symbolic link to the system password file.

See also: Race condition.

**Transport Layer Security (TLS)**

The successor to SSL, a protocol for establishing secure channels over a reliable transport, using a standard X.509 Public Key Infrastructure for authenticating machines. The protocol is standardized by the IETF.

See also: Secure Socket Layer.

**Triple DES**

A variant of the original Data Encryption Standard that doubles the effective security. Often abbreviated to 3DES. The security level of 3DES is still considered to be very high, but there are faster block ciphers that provide comparable levels of security — such as AES.

See also: Data Encryption Standard.

**Trojan**

See also: Backdoor.

**Trojan Horse**

See also: Backdoor.

**Trusted third party**

An entity in a system to whom entities must extend some implicit trust. For example, in a typical Public Key Infrastructure, the Certification Authority constitutes a trusted third party.

**Twofish**

A modern block cipher with 128-bit blocks and variable-sized keys. A finalist in the AES competition; it is an evolution of the Blowfish cipher.

See also: AES, Blowfish.

**U**

**UMAC**

A secure MAC based on a set of universal hash functions that is extremely fast in software but so complex that there has never been a validated implementation.

See also: Universal hash function.

**Universal hash function**

A keyed hash function that has ideal hash properties. In practice, the only practical functions of this nature are really "almost universal" hash functions, meaning they come very close to being ideal. Universal and near-universal hash functions are not cryptographically secure when used naively for message authentication but can be adapted to be secure for this purpose easily.

See also: Cryptographic hash function, Hash function, One-way hash function.

**V**

**Validation**

The act of determining that data is sound. In security, generally used in the context of validating input.

**VMAC**

Variant of UMAC optimized for 64-bit architectures.

See also: UMAC.

# W

## Weak collision resistance

A property that a hash function may have (and a good cryptographic hash function will have), characterized by it being unfeasible to find a second input that produces the same output as a known input.

See also: Hash function, Strong collision resistance.

## Whitelist

When performing input validation, the set of items that, if matched, results in the input being accepted as valid. If there is no match to the whitelist, then the input is considered invalid. That is, a whitelist uses a "default deny" policy.

See also: Blacklist, Default deny.

## Window of vulnerability

The period of time in which a vulnerability can possibly be exploited.

# X

## X.509 certificate

A digital certificate that complies with the X.509 standard (produced by ANSI).

## XCBC-MAC

A three-key variant of the CBC-MAC that overcomes the fundamental limitation of that MAC.

See also: Message Authentication Code, CBC-MAC, OMAC.

## XMACC

A patented parallelizable Message Authentication Code.

**XSS**

See also: Cross-site scripting.

H/t OWASP Shared under Attribution-ShareAlike 4.0 International (CC BY-SA 4.0)

## Special Thanks

-Ed Skoudis – your leadership, wisdom, and friendship has been invaluable to me, thank you.

-Joshua Wright – "Hey this guy teaching this course is pretty smart. Oh wow…he wrote all these tools I've been using for years…"

-The SANS Admin team, in no particular order, Karyn Adam, Bette-Lou Brown, Shelley Wark-Martyn, Deanna Boyden, Larry Dudak, Rob Lee, and Andrea Ericsson. Sorry if I missed anyone!

-The SANS Advisory board for suggesting some excellent quotes, including Patrick Glynn, Doug Metz, Michael Jacobs, Christopher Hamilton, Colin Hart, Robert Kirtley, and Edwin Martinez II.

Lightning Source UK Ltd.
Milton Keynes UK
UKHW021422030720
365983UK00004B/312